An Amnesty International Report

POLITICAL IMPRISONMENT IN THE PEOPLE'S REPUBLIC OF CHINA

AMNESTY INTERNATIONAL is a worldwide movement which is independent of any government, political grouping, ideology, economic interest or religious creed. It plays a specific role within the overall spectrum of human rights work. The activities of the organization focus strictly on prisoners:

- It seeks the *release* of men and women detained anywhere for their beliefs, colour, sex, ethnic origin, language or religion, provided they have neither used nor advocated violence. These are termed *'prisoners of conscience'*.
- It advocates *fair and early trials* for *all political prisoners* and works on behalf of such persons detained without charge or without trial.
- It opposes the *death penalty* and *torture* or other cruel, inhuman or degrading treatment or punishment of *all prisoners* without reservation.

AMNESTY INTERNATIONAL acts on the basis of the United Nations Universal Declaration of Human Rights and other international instruments. Through practical work for prisoners within its mandate, Amnesty International participates in the wider promotion and protection of human rights in the civil, political, economic, social and cultural spheres.

AMNESTY INTERNATIONAL has over 2,000 adoption groups and national sections in 35 countries in Africa, Asia, Europe, the Americas and the Middle East, and individual members in a further 74 countries. Each adoption group works for at least two prisoners of conscience in countries other than its own. These countries are balanced geographically and politically to ensure impartiality. Information about prisoners and human rights violations emanates from Amnesty International's Research Department in London.

AMNESTY INTERNATIONAL has consultative status with the United Nations (ECOSOC), UNESCO and the Council of Europe, has cooperative relations with the Inter-American Commission on Human Rights of the Organization of American States and has observer status with the Organization of African Unity (Bureau for the Placement and Education of African Refugees).

AMNESTY INTERNATIONAL is financed by subscriptions and donations of its worldwide membership. To safeguard the independence of the organization, all contributions are strictly controlled by guidelines laid down by AI's International Council and income and expenditure are made public in an annual financial report.

An Amnesty International Report

POLITICAL IMPRISONMENT IN THE PEOPLE'S REPUBLIC OF CHINA

AMNESTY INTERNATIONAL PUBLICATIONS

First published 1978 by Amnesty International Publications,
10 Southampton Street, London WC2E 7HF, England
Copyright © Amnesty International Publications
ISBN 0-394-73719-9
AI Index: PUB 101/00/78
Original language: English
Printed in the United States of America.

ACKNOWLEDGEMENTS

Amnesty International makes grateful acknowledgement to
the following publishers for their permission to quote from
the works listed below:

Coward, McCann and Geoghegan Inc., New York:
Prisoner of Mao by Bao Ruowang (Jean Pasqualini) and
Rudolph Chelminski

Fred B. Rothman and Co., Littleton, Colorado:
Fundamental Legal Documents of Communist China by
Albert Blaustein

Harvard University Press, Cambridge, Mass.:
The Criminal Process in the People's Republic of China
by Jerome Alan Cohen

Congrès pour la Liberté de la Culture, Paris:
The Hundred Flowers by Roderick MacFarquhar

Amnesty International thanks the British Broadcasting
Corporation's Monitoring Service also for permission to
quote extracts from the Summary of World Broadcasts
(Far East).

Contents

Preface

Since 1977 the Chinese official press has publicized a number of cases where violations of human rights committed in the People's Republic of China (PRC) during the past ten years have been redressed. Amnesty International welcomes these measures; it also welcomes a decision reported to have been adopted in spring 1978 by the Chinese People's Political Consultative Conference on the release of, or restoration of rights to, thousands of people who had been classified as "rightists" since 1957. However, Amnesty International is concerned by the fact that arrests on political grounds are continuing and that the legislation permitting imprisonment on such grounds is still operative.

An article in the Chinese newspaper the *People's Daily* of 13 July 1978 indicated that changes in the legislation are being considered: the article stated that the country needed a "criminal code", a "civil code" and a set of "rules of legal procedure" on the basis of which the "masses of the people" could "institute legal proceedings under the law so as to protect their legitimate interests". Amnesty International welcomes these proposals and would also welcome positive measures which the Government might take towards an overall review of the laws and procedures affecting political offenders.

During the past few years, Amnesty International has addressed appeals and inquiries to the authorities in the PRC about cases of prisoners of conscience, arrests and death penalties—including reported executions of political offenders—in the country. On several occasions Amnesty International stressed its wish to discuss these cases and other matters of concern with representatives of the Government of the People's Republic of China. However, all appeals and inquiries, as well as requests to meet representatives of the Government, have met with no response.

In May 1978, the Chairman of the International Executive Committee of Amnesty International, Thomas Hammarberg, wrote to the Ambassador of the PRC in Sweden, His Excellency Chin Li-chen, informing him that Amnesty International had prepared a report on aspects of the legislation and penal practice in the PRC which were of particular concern to it. The letter indicated that Amnesty International wished to submit this report to the Government and proposed an interview with the Ambassador.

On 13 June 1978 the typescript of Amnesty International's *Report on Political Imprisonment in the People's Republic of China* was transmitted to the Embassy of the PRC in Stockholm for submission to the Government. In a covering letter, Amnesty International said that it would welcome comments on the report, as well as an opportunity of discussing the matters raised in it with representatives of the Government of the People's Republic of China.

By mid-August 1978 no comments or replies had been received from the authorities of the PRC. On 18 August 1978 the International Executive Committee of Amnesty International decided to publish this report, which reflects the organization's concern at imprisonment for political reasons in the PRC. The International Executive Committee emphasized that it would still welcome any corrections to or comments on the facts presented in the report from the Government of the People's Republic of China.

Introduction

This report describes the major aspects of political imprisonment in the People's Republic of China (PRC)—the laws providing for imprisonment on political grounds, the judicial process and prison conditions.

The report examines in particular the published laws of the PRC relating to political imprisonment and the conditions in which political offenders—whether or not they are convicted—are detained. It notes that the legal provisions defining political offences are loosely worded and have been interpreted broadly, permitting large-scale imprisonment on political grounds, and that the Constitution and other official documents also provide that certain categories of people—defined as "class enemies"—are deprived of their political and civil rights on the basis of their "class origin" or political background.

The report also notes that the law has increasingly played a minor role since the late 1950s due to continuing "mass mobilization campaigns" which are used as a means both of mass education and of identifying offenders, including people dissenting from official policy. These campaigns have contributed to broadening the range of political offences to the extent that each of them has defined new types of offenders according to the political necessities of the period. Formal legal procedures have often been neglected during such campaigns, particularly between 1966 and 1976.

The law thus reflects only some aspects of the policy followed towards political offenders in the People's Republic of China. This is also true of the penalties imposed on political offenders. Apart from "formal" penalties, ranging from a term of imprisonment to the death penalty, there are also "informal" or "administrative" sanctions which do not require judicial investigation or other legal process. The offenders affected by these "non-criminal" sanctions are not brought before a court of justice, but, for punishments such as "work under supervision" or "rehabilitation through labour", they are assigned, as convicted prisoners are, to compulsory labour under special control (see p. 5) either in society or in penal establishments.

The report criticizes the practice of detaining political offenders for long periods before trial and the lack of formal guarantees of their right to defence. According to the law, pre-trial detention may be unlimited once an "arrest warrant" has been issued by the police (Public Security) and is often used to compel offenders to write confessions before they are brought to trial. Political defendants are usually tried *in camera* or, in some cases, through "mass public trials" where no defence is possible. The right to defence is generally limited by the fact that non-admission of guilt is officially regarded as an aggravating circumstance when judgment is passed.

The report also describes some aspects of detention conditions which fall below the national standards prescribed by Chinese law for the maintenance of prisoners and do not conform to the United Nations Standard Minimum Rules for the Treatment of Prisoners regarding the rights and treatment of individual prisoners. Although the information on prison conditions in this report is limited to particular penal establishments and periods—up to 1976—there are aspects of detention conditions which have, over the years, been the object of constant complaints by political prisoners—in particular the system of punishment. While all the penal establishments mentioned in the report held both "ordinary" criminal and political offenders, there is evidence that the latter are liable to be treated more severely because their attitude during their detention is questioned in the light of their political background.

It must be emphasized, however, that the report is not meant to present a picture of the conditions of detention prevailing in the whole of the country at any particular moment. The lack of detailed information on political imprisonment in the People's Republic of China is due to various factors, including the size and diversity of the country, the complexity of the issues involved in the handling of political offenders, the restriction of movement and the lack of free access to information. Nevertheless, official documents alone present sufficient evidence that the treatment of political offenders results from a consistent policy of denying to individuals the right to deviate from standards of behaviour defined by official policy.

While the information available on current individual cases of prisoners of conscience in the PRC is limited, the report does present examples of people either temporarily detained or sentenced for exercising their right to hold and express their beliefs.

Amnesty International's primary concern is for the release of all prisoners of conscience. It welcomes the provisions of the 1978 Constitution of the PRC designed to safeguard the rights of citizens, but notes that the new Constitution—as well as the existing criminal laws—also contains provisions which violate the fundamental human rights of individual citizens and permit imprisonment on political grounds. Amnesty International would welcome any steps on the part of the Government of the People's Republic of China towards signing and ratifying the United Nations International Covenant on Civil and Political Rights, to guarantee to its citizens their fundamental human rights and to safeguard these rights by appropriate judicial procedures.

The information in this report is based on two main sources: official published documents and accounts by former prisoners and refugees. The legal texts and other official documents which are available provide essential information on the official principles and institutions related to the penal policy of the PRC. The published laws quoted in this report constitute to date the country's main criminal laws. They are available in two collections published in Peking in the 1950s: *Zhonghua Renmin Gongheguo Fagui Huipian*** (Collection of Laws and Regulations of the People's Republic of China) and *Zhongyang Renmin Zhengfu Faling Huipian* (Collection of Laws and Ordinances of the Central People's Government). Various translations of the laws exist and this report mainly follows that of Jerome Alan Cohen in *The Criminal Process in the People's Republic of China, 1949-1963: An Introduction* (Harvard, Cambridge, Mass., 1968).

Official documents, however, provide little information on individual cases of political offenders and their treatment. Actual details have been obtained mainly from statements by former detainees and prisoners, by their acquaintances or by refugees familiar with aspects of the legal process described in the report. As stressed earlier, these sources also have limitations in that they generally provide a partial picture of a complex process. It can also be objected that they may be biased. However, the accounts of various people who do not know each other and who come from different places in China often present the same picture of a particular event and penal practice, and can sometimes be further corroborated by official documents or statements. Although some details are difficult to check, such accounts present a pattern in various aspects of political imprisonment which is to a large extent confirmed by official documents; taken as a whole, they can therefore be regarded as convincing testimonies.

Amnesty International believes that respect for human rights should be a matter of international observance and responsibility. It would welcome comments from the authorities of the People's Republic of China on the facts presented in this report and their interpretation, as well as any steps they may take to safeguard the fundamental human rights of individual citizens.

*See Note on Transcription and Abbreviations, p. xiv.

NOTE ON TRANSCRIPTION AND ABBREVIATIONS

Transcriptions

With some exceptions (see below), the names of people and places in this report have been transcribed according to the official romanization system of the People's Republic of China—the *pinyin zimu*. Various other transcription systems exist, in Britain, France, Germany and other countries. Some examples of the different transcriptions in the current British system and in the Chinese *pinyin zimu* system are given below:

English transcription	*pinyin zimu*
Names of people:	
Cheng Chao-lin	Zheng Chaolin
Chiang Ching	Jiang Qing
Chiang Kai-shek	Jiang Jieshi
Chou En-lai	Zhou Enlai
Hua Kuo-feng	Hua Guofeng
Li Cheng-tien	Li Zhengtian
Lin Hsi-ling	Lin Xiling
Lin Piao	Lin Biao
Liu Shao-chi	Liu Shaoqi
Mao Tse-tung (or Mao Tsetung)	Mao Zedong
Teng Ching-shan	Deng Qingshan
Wang Ming-tao	Wang Mingdao
Yeh Chien-ying	Ye Jianying
Names of places:	
Chengtu (city)	Chengdu
Chinghai (province)	Qinghai
Chungking (city)	Zhongqing
Hangchow (city)	Hangzhou
Hankow (city)	Hankou
Heilungkiang (province)	Heilongjiang
Honan (province)	Henan
Hopei (province)	Hebei
Hupei (province)	Hubei

English transcription	*pinyin zimu*

Names of places:

Kansu (province)	Gansu
Kiangsi (province)	Jiangxi
Kiangsu (province)	Jiangsu
Kirin (province)	Jilin
Kwangchow (city) or Canton	Guangzhou
Kwangtung (province)	Guangdong
Kwangsi (province)	Guangxi
Nanking (city)	Nanjing
Ninghsia (province)	Ningxia
Peking (city)	Beijing
Shansi (province)	Shānxi
Shensi (province)	Shǎnxi
Sinkiang (province)	Xinjiang
Szechuan (province)	Sichuan
Tientsin (city)	Tianjin

In two cases, the transcriptions "Mao Tsetung" and "Peking" have been used throughout the text rather than the equivalent transcriptions in the *pinyin zimu* system. In addition, the Chinese characters for names mentioned in the report were not always available. In such cases, the transcription used in the report is the one which appeared in the original text where the names were mentioned.

Most Chinese names are composed of three syllables—for example, Deng Qingshan—the first of which is the surname (Deng) and the two others the given name (Qingshan). In this report, we have often referred to a person by his/her surname (in this case, Deng), once the full name has been mentioned.

Abbreviations

The most common abbreviations mentioned in the report are the following:

PRC:	People's Republic of China
CCP:	Chinese Communist Party
CC:	Central Committee
NPC:	National People's Congress
PLA:	People's Liberation Army
NCNA:	New China News Agency
SWB:	Summary of World Broadcasts (published by the monitoring service of the British Broadcasting Corporation)

The Law and the Concept of Political Offence

Official reference to political offenders in the People's Republic of China can easily be found in the official press and documents. However, they are usually called "counter-revolutionaries", a term which refers to people charged with a broad range of political offences, including offences of opinion. In 1960, Edgar Snow, one of the few foreigners who were, at that time, allowed to visit Chinese prisons, was told that the main prison in Peking accommodated forty per cent "counter-revolutionaries" out of a total of 1,800 inmates. Many of them had been imprisoned since 1949. He learned also that a detention center adjacent to the main prison held between two and four hundred political prisoners "for interrogation and thought reform", prior to trial.[1]

A number of laws adopted in the first decade of the People's Republic of China (1949-59) specifically provide for arrest and imprisonment on political grounds, and the country's Constitution includes provisions limiting civil liberties and depriving certain categories of people of their political and civil rights.

Some of the laws published in the 1950s were still in force in 1977. The existing published laws are, however, insufficient to indicate the range of political offences and of their punishments; as will be seen later, they give a loose definition of political offences and can be interpreted broadly. Chinese judges interviewed by foreign visitors have stated that law is not the only factor determining the handling of cases. Political considerations have always been taken into account in the treatment of offenders and this trend has become more marked since the Cultural Revolution (1966-68). Thus, strict interpretation of the law is not of primary importance in judicial work and law is mainly used to enforce official policy. When defendants are sentenced, the official announcements of the judgment generally do not refer to the relevant law and provisions permitting the punishment, but simply state that they have been punished "according to the law".

Whereas the law gives only a general idea of what constitutes a political offence, other official texts help in understanding the policy towards political offenders. They show that anyone who dissents from official policy is liable to be punished in various ways, including imprisonment, and that some social groups are more likely than others to become the object of repression. This chapter will examine the legislation providing for detention on political grounds and other relevant texts.

Political offences in legal and other official documents

The People's Republic of China (PRC) has no criminal or civil code and only a few laws have been published since 1949. The main legal documents[2] relevant to political offenders are the following:

- The Constitution of the PRC, 1954, amended 1975 and 1978
- The Act of the PRC for Punishment of Counter-revolution, 1951
- The Provisional Measures of the PRC for the Control of Counter-revolutionaries, 1952
- The Act of the PRC for Reform Through Labour, 1954
- The Provisional Measures of the PRC for dealing with the Release of Reform Through Labour Criminals at the Expiration of Their Term of Imprisonment and for Placing Them and Getting Them Employment, 1954
- The Arrest and Detention Act of the PRC, 1954
- The Decision of the Standing Committee of the National People's Congress of the PRC Relating to Control of Counter-revolutionaries in All Cases Being Decided Upon by Judgment of a People's Court, 1956
- The Decision of the State Council of the PRC Relating to Problems of Rehabilitation Through Labour, 1957

The laws and documents examined below are those which deal with deprivation of rights and political offences. The other laws listed above are mentioned in later chapters.

A revised text of the Constitution of the PRC was adopted on 5 March 1978 by the Fifth National People's Congress of the PRC. Like the Constitutions of 1954 and 1975, it includes a chapter on the "Fundamental Rights and Duties of Citizens". Article 45 of the new Constitution guarantees a number of basic rights, such as "freedom of speech, correspondence, the press, assembly, association, procession, demonstration and the freedom to strike"[3] and stipulates that citizens have the right to "speak out freely, air their views fully, hold great debates and write big-character posters". "Freedom to believe in religion" is guaranteed in Article 46. Article 14 also includes a paragraph indicative of a certain liberalization in the field of arts and sciences:

"The State applies the principle of 'letting a hundred flowers blossom and a hundred schools of thought contend' so as to promote the development of the arts and sciences and bring about a flourishing socialist culture."

This, however, is restricted by another provision in the same Article:

"The State upholds the leading position of Marxism-Leninism-Mao Tsetung-Thought in all spheres of ideology and culture. All cultural undertakings must serve the workers, peasants and soldiers and serve socialism."

Other articles of the 1978 Constitution include provisions limiting fundamental freedoms, in particular Article 56:

"Citizens must support the leadership of the Chinese Communist Party, support the socialist system, safeguard the unification of the motherland and the unity of all nationalities in our country and abide by the Constitution and the law."

Article 46 states that the citizens enjoy "freedom to believe in religion", but it is not clear whether or not this includes the right to *practice* religion. The Article omits the right to propagate religion whereas it specifically guarantees "freedom not to believe in religion and to propagate atheism".

Article 18 provides for punishment of political offenders and for deprivation of rights for certain categories of people:

"The State safeguards the socialist system, suppresses all treasonable and counter-revolutionary activities, punishes all traitors and counter-revolutionaries, and punishes newborn bourgeois elements and other bad elements.

"The State deprives of political rights, as prescribed by law, those landlords, rich peasants and reactionary capitalists who have not yet been reformed, and at the same time it provides them with the opportunity to earn a living so that they may be reformed through labour and become law-abiding citizens supporting themselves by their own labour."

This Article reveals the continuity of official policy vis-à-vis political offenders: it is a modified version of Article 7 of the Common Program adopted on 29 September 1949 by the Chinese People's Political Consultative Conference, on the eve of the proclamation of the People's Republic of China. All the old laws of the Nationalist Government were abrogated at the same time and the Common Program served as a provisional constitution until the National People's Congress adopted a Constitution in 1954.

Article 7 of the Common Program also inspired the first law affecting political offenders drawn up by the new Government: the Act of the PRC for Punishment of Counter-revolution. Passed on 20 February 1951 and promulgated the next day, it is one of the main criminal laws of the People's Republic of China. It was still in force in 1977 and was mentioned in the official press as one of the main laws of the country.[4]

Article 2 of the Act defines in general terms offenders punishable under the Act as "all counter-revolutionary criminals whose goal is to overthrow the people's democratic régime or to undermine the undertaking of the people's democracy".

Articles 3, 4, 5, 6 and 9 of the Act provide penalties for acts or intention to commit acts endangering the security of the state: treason, insurrection, incitement to insurrection, espionage, sabotage, etc. Other articles illustrate the broad meaning given to the expression "to undermine the undertaking of the people's democracy".

Article 10 in particular stipulates that those who, "with a counter-revolutionary purpose", provoke "dissension among the various nationalities, democratic classes, democratic parties and groups, people's organizations or between the people and the government" (paragraph 2), or who conduct "counter-revolutionary propaganda and agitation" and create and spread rumours (paragraph 3), shall be punished by no less than three years' imprisonment, or by death or life imprisonment when the "circumstances of their cases are major".

The law is no more specific about what is meant by, for instance, "provoking dissension . . . between the people and the government" or "spreading rumours" or committing such offences "with a counter-revolutionary purpose". With this loose formulation, Article 10 can apply to a wide range of offences of opinion which can be punished by anything from three years' imprisonment to the death penalty, depending on the "circumstances of the case".

The same looseness can be found in other articles. For instance, the Act also provides for the punishment of people who "with a counter-revolutionary purpose, secretly cross the borders of the state" (Article 11); who "harbour or conceal counter-revolutionary criminals" (Article 12); who before 1949 participated in "organizations of counter-revolutionary secret agents or spies" if, since liberation, they have continued to "participate in counter-revolutionary activity" or to "link themselves" with counter-revolutionary secret agents and spies (Article 7).

All offences listed in the Act may be punished by death or life imprisonment, in some cases with the stipulation "where the circumstances of the cases are major", and some articles specify minimum terms of imprisonment. However, Article 14 stipulates that those who "voluntarily surrender and repent" or "atone for their crimes" or committed these "crimes" involuntarily or through coercion may be given reduced punishment or be exempted from punishment.

This law is applicable retroactively to people who had committed "counter-revolutionary" offences before the Act was promulgated (Article 18). Moreover, Article 16 provides that "crimes committed with a counter-revolutionary purpose" which are not covered by the Act may be punished in the same way as those listed in the Act to which they are comparable. This is another example of the looseness of the law.

In 1952 the Government adopted regulations for the "control" of "counter-revolutionaries" which supplemented the 1951 Act for Punishment of Counter-revolution. These regulations were entitled "Provisional Measures of the PRC for Control of Counter-revolutionaries".[5] The stated aim of the Measures was "to give counter-revolutionaries definite punishment and ideological education to enable them to reform into new persons" by putting them to work "under control of the Government and supervision by the masses" (Article 2).

The provisions for "control" are still in force, but have been slightly modified since their promulgation.[6] "Control" means a forcible assignment to work under surveillance, but this assignment can be carried out in society. According to the Provisional Measures, "control" was to apply to "historical counter-revolutionaries", that is, people considered deserving of punishment by the new régime because of their actions or social position under the previous Government (before 1949). In the terms of the Provisional Measures, "though they have not engaged in current counter-revolutionary activity" (that is, though they have not committed "crimes" since 1949), they "must be given definite punishment" if they have not "demonstrated or proved their repentance and reform" (Article 3). The Measures further indicate that those "historical counter-revolutionaries" who should be "controlled" are those whose "evil acts" were not such that they had to be arrested and sentenced. They are listed as follows in Article 3 of the Provisional Measures:

1. counter-revolutionary secret agents;
2. backbone elements of reactionary parties and youth leagues;
3. heads of reactionary societies;
4. landlord elements who persist in their reactionary standpoint;
5. Chiang [Kai-shek]'s counterfeit military and government officials who persist in their reactionary standpoint;

6. other counter-revolutionaries who should be controlled.

According to the Provisional Measures, "controlled elements" shall be deprived of political and civil rights (Article 4) and anyone shall have the right "to supervise controlled elements and to denounce their unlawful activity" (Article 10). However, only the individuals concerned are to be "controlled"; "members of their families, relatives and friends may not be involved" (Article 9). "Control" shall last no more than three years, but may be extended "when necessary" (Article 6).

The term "crime" is not used in these Measures, which provided for people to be punished by "control" for "evil acts" committed before the establishment of the PRC. As will be seen later,[7] "control" was made a formal criminal punishment in 1956, but as defined in the 1952 Provisional Measures it was imposed on people who were not convicted of a "crime".

When the Act for Punishment of Counter-revolution and the Provisional Measures for Control of Counter-revolutionaries were adopted, the Land Reform was already under way in China. A national campaign to "suppress counter-revolutionaries" was launched concurrently between 1951 and 1952. The arrests made during that period affected for the most part the former privileged classes in rural and urban areas as well as people accused of owing "blood-debts" to the people.

The search for counter-revolutionaries did not stop with the completion of the Land Reform. Arrests continued throughout the following years during other mobilization campaigns. It was later officially admitted that a number of "mistakes" had been made in the process.[8] In June 1956, the then Minister of Public Security, Luo Ruiqing, presented a report on the repression of counter-revolutionaries to the Third Session of the National People's Congress.[9] He admitted in it that "a small number of elements that need not have been arrested had been arrested". Stressing the importance of following the Party and Government leadership in order to avoid mistakes, the Minister also said: ". . . torture and forced confessions during interrogation must be strictly prevented; one must carry out properly the work of investigation and research, attach importance to evidence and not believe lightly in statements . . ." Luo Ruiqing concluded by declaring: "As long as there are counter-revolutionary elements and counter-revolutionary sabotage activities, we are determined to carry on the struggle against counter-revolutionary elements to the very end . . ."

Chairman Mao himself, in a speech made in April 1956,[10] affirmed that the past campaigns of suppression of counter-revolutionaries and the executions carried out in the process had been necessary.[11] He emphasized that there were still "a small number" of counter-revolutionaries carrying out "sabotage",[12] but that from then on there should be fewer arrests and executions.

The laws described above are still in force as of 1977, and new laws and regulations affecting political offenders have been added, as will be seen below. They are so broadly phrased as to make them applicable to any opponents of those in power, depending on the current policy line.

Policy principles: The theory of the class struggle

The principles underlying the policy on the suppression of counter-revolutionaries were outlined by Mao Tsetung before the establishment of the People's Republic of China. They were based on the theory that the abolition of private property, of privileges and classes would ultimately lead to the establishment of a communist society where "all instruments of class struggle—parties and the state machinery" would naturally disappear.[13] In his view, the way to achieve this was to establish a monopoly of power for the party representing the proletariat—the Communist Party—and to deprive of their rights all "reactionary" individuals and groups threatening this power. The "reactionaries" would therefore be punished if they spoke or acted in a way prejudicial to the people's dictatorship.

The text "On the People's Democratic Dictatorship", written by Mao Tsetung for the commemoration of the twenty-eighth anniversary of the Chinese Communist Party (CCP) on 30 June 1949, is explicit on this question. In it Mao declared that the conditions in which to achieve the ultimate goal of the abolition of classes in Chinese society are "the leadership of the Communist Party and the state power of the people's dictatorship". He explained in some detail the meaning of the enforcement of the "people's dictatorship":

> "All the experience the Chinese people have accumulated through several decades teaches us to enforce the people's democratic dictatorship, that is, to deprive the reactionaries of the right to speak and let the people alone have that right.
>
> "Who are the people? At the present stage in China, they are the working class, the peasantry, the urban petty bourgeoisie and the national bourgeoisie. These classes, led by the working class and the Communist Party, unite to form their own state and elect their own government; they enforce their dictatorship over the running dogs of imperialism—the landlord class and bureaucrat-bourgeoisie, as well as the representatives of those

classes, the Guomindang [Nationalist Party] reactionaries and their accomplices—suppress them, allow them only to behave themselves and not to be unruly in word or deed. If they speak or act in an unruly way, they will be promptly stopped and punished. Democracy is practised within the ranks of the people, who enjoy the rights of freedom of speech, assembly, association and so on. The right to vote belongs only to the people, not to the reactionaries. The combination of these two aspects, democracy for the people and the dictatorship over the reactionaries, is the people's democratic dictatorship."

Mao also said that "the state apparatus, including the army, the police and the courts, is the instrument by which one class oppresses another. It is an instrument for the oppression of antagonistic classes; it is violence and not 'benevolence'."

"Benevolence" was to be applied only to the "people", who still had to free themselves of all "reactionary" influences. "Benevolence towards the people" meant that the people had to be educated through persuasion and not compulsion, unlike the reactionaries. However, Mao already foresaw that the national bourgeoisie, which in 1949 was still reckoned to be in the ranks of the people, would be educated and remoulded "a step further" when the time came to nationalize private enterprise. This became a reality in 1952 when Mao declared: "With the overthrow of the landlord class and the bureaucrat-capitalist class, the contradiction between the working class and the national bourgeoisie has become the principal contradiction in China; therefore the national bourgeoisie should no longer be defined as an intermediate class".[14]

During the following years, the "people's democratic dictatorship" became the "dictatorship of the proletariat". In 1957 Mao presented an elaborated theory of the "class struggle" in his talk "On the Correct Handling of Contradictions Among the People".[15] The arguments in this talk are still determining factors in the treatment of political offenders.

The basic premise of Mao's analysis was that classes still exist after the victory of the socialist revolution and that "class struggle" continues throughout the period of "socialist construction". The continued existence of classes means that there is still a danger of capitalist restoration, which can be avoided only by a proper handling of the two main types of contradictions in society. First, there are contradictions (conflicts) of an ideological nature "within the ranks of the people": for instance, various interests may oppose workers and peasants, the peasantry and the intelligentsia, the state and the individual, etc. But these contradictions can be resolved by "criticism, persuasion and education" and by "administrative regulations", because the classes and social groups belonging to the "people" are those who "support and work for socialist construction".

There are also contradictions between "ourselves" (the people) and "the enemy" which are antagonistic in nature. The "enemies" are defined as the "social forces and groups which resist the socialist revolution and are hostile to or sabotage socialist construction". The way to deal with the "enemies" is to submit them to the "dictatorship". Mao explained: "For instance, to arrest, try and sentence certain counter-revolutionaries, and to deprive landlords and bureaucrat-capitalists of their right to vote and their freedom of speech for a certain period of time—all this comes within the scope of our dictatorship."

Moreover, Mao declared earlier in this text that the concept of "the people" varies in different periods of history in a given country. This argument puts into a broader perspective the policy of repression of political dissent, as it implies that anyone can in fact become the "object of the dictatorship"—in other words, be deprived of freedom— depending on the political necessities of the period.

The importance of the "class struggle" and of the differentiation of classes is stressed daily in China and the official press carries numerous articles on the subject. The new Constitution adopted in March 1978 stresses, in its preamble, that the class struggle must be continued: ". . . the general task for the people of the whole country in this new period is to persevere in continuing the revolution under the dictatorship of the proletariat, carry forward the three great revolutionary movements of class struggle, the struggle for production, and scientific experiment . . ." The categories traditionally singled out as the "class enemies" among the population are: the "landlords", "rich peasants", "counter-revolutionaries", "bad elements" and "rightists".

These categories are called in China the "five categories of elements" or more commonly the "five bad elements". The first three categories—"landlords", "rich peasants", and "counter-revolutionaries"—were the targets of the 1950/52 campaigns for the Land Reform and for the Suppression of Counter-revolutionaries and of the 1953/55 campaigns against counter-revolutionaries. The fourth category, "bad elements", refers to common-law criminals and petty offenders. It is a catch-all term used to designate people regarded as exhibiting improper social behaviour; it is also sometimes used as a generic term for all the other categories. The fifth category, "rightists", appeared in 1957 to designate members of the intelligentsia who had voiced criticism of the Party during the "Hundred Flowers" movement.[16] These categories still exist, although the "rightists" are now rarely mentioned among "class enemies". On the other hand, the 1978 Constitution introduced in Article 18 a new category of class enemies: the "new-born bourgeois elements". A definition of this new category was given by Marshal Ye Jianying on 1 March 1978: "It refers to those newly emerged elements who resist socialist revolution, disrupt socialist construction, gravely undermine socialist public ownership, appropriate social property or violate the criminal law."[17] In other words, they may be people held on political grounds, or for "economic" or common-law offences. Marshal Ye Jianying also stated: ". . . the punishment for new-born bourgeois elements has been added in conformity with the present situation of the class struggle in our country."

Anyone classified in one of these categories is, according to Chinese terminology, given a "cap" (*mao*), and is referred to figuratively as "wearing a cap" (*dai mao*). To be given a label (or "cap") means, at least, to be deprived of political (i.e., civil) rights and to be put under some form of control. It can also mean arrest and imprisonment. Moreover, whatever the nature and the length of the punishment, the social stigma attached to such labels may affect the victims for the rest of their lives. It may also extend to their family dependants if their political attitude is questioned, as family background is invariably taken into account in such cases.

An article in the official paper, the *People's Daily*, of 18 February 1978, criticized the practice of discriminating against the family of someone in disfavour. It pointed out in particular that children whose parents have "seriously questionable backgrounds" or "serious political problems" should not be involved. However, the article also stressed that "importance should be attached to the theory of class origin and political behaviour, but not to the theory of class origin alone". This shows that class origin is still considered important if "political behaviour" is judged unsatisfactory.

The importance of class background

As seen earlier, the Constitution and law provide that people having a certain class origin or political background shall be deprived of their political rights "as prescribed by law" if they have "not yet reformed" and shall be subjected to the punishment known as "control" if they persist in their "reactionary standpoint". This applies particularly to members of the former "landlord", "rich peasant" and "reactionary capitalist" classes.

Everyone in China has both a "class origin" and a "class status". Family (or class) background constitutes the "class origin" of an individual; "class status" is determined by a person's work.

In 1950, the Government adopted Decisions[18] which gave specific guidelines for determining class status. For instance, the intelligentsia was not considered a class in itself:

"The class origin of intellectuals is to be determined according to the status of their families. The class status of the intellectuals themselves is to be determined in accordance with the means they employ to earn the major part of their income."[19]

According to the Decisions, a man of landlord or rich peasant origin who has become a worker after 1949 has the class status of "worker". His wife and children shall also have the status of "workers", but the other members of his family "shall be treated as landlords or rich peasants in status".[20] This man's "class origin", however, is still the same and, since landlords and rich peasants belong to the "bad" classes, this may be held against him at any time if his political loyalty is questioned.

Direct dependants inherit their "class status" from the head of the family. If the father dies, a child or teenager will take the class status of the next senior person in the family and be treated accordingly. In addition, if the child's father has been a landlord under the previous régime and if, for some reason, the father's class designation has not been changed, the child retains a "landlord status" until he or she finds employment. The conditions necessary for changing the class status of landlords and rich peasants were laid down in the Decisions:

"Landlords who, since the completion of the agrarian reform, have always obeyed the Government's laws and decrees, devoted themselves strenuously to labour and production or other occupations and have not been found guilty of any reactionary conduct whatsoever for over five consecutive years, may have their class status changed to that of labourers or others according to the nature of the labour or occupation they have engaged in, by decision of the *hsiang* people's representative conference and with the approval of the county people's government.[21] . . .The rich peasants in the old liberated areas,[22] who have conformed to the foregoing conditions for three years since the completion of agrarian reform, may have their class status changed in the same way. Those who have failed to conform to the foregoing conditions should not have their class status changed."[23]

Class background becomes particularly important during the mass "mobilization" campaigns which are launched periodically in China.

Such campaigns are used for many purposes: to deter crime, corruption, waste and black marketeering; for the political and economic mobilization of the population; and for political purification. During a campaign, increased emphasis is given to the class struggle and the search for "class enemies" is more intense than usual. Whatever the purpose of the campaign, people who have a "bad" class status or origin are generally the first to be scrutinized in the process.[24]

A Chinese language review published in Hong Kong, *Huang He*,[25] recently gave the example of one case where class status was an important factor in arrest during the 1970 "one-strike three-anti" (*yida sanfan*) campaign. This purification campaign was carried out while Lin Biao (Lin Piao) was still in power as Vice-Chairman of the Party. It had both a political and an economic purpose: "one-strike" meant to strike against "counter-revolutionaries according to present activities",[26] "three-anti" meant to struggle against corruption, waste and the black market. According to the review *Huang He*, a 26-year-old man named Deng Qingshan was arrested in a rural production brigade during this campaign and falsely accused of slandering Chairman Mao.

Deng Qingshan had lost his mother while he was still very young and his father had died after the Land Reform. Deng's father had "poor peasant" status and had been an active "red element" during the Land Reform. After his death, the head of the family was Deng's older brother, who had fought in the Korean War and through this had gained the prestige of the "revolutionary fighters". Because of this good background, Deng's childhood was protected. He was able to attend middle-school classes and in 1963 he was preparing to enter university. However, an important event affected his brother at that time. After his return from the Korean War, Deng's brother had differences of opinion with the cadres of the production brigade and his relationship with them soon became very tense. In 1963, during a campaign to "afforest the country", the cadres seized the pretext that the brother had gone to chop wood to accuse him of "undermining" this campaign and labelled him a "bad element". Deng's life was immediately affected by his brother's fate. He was not admitted to university and returned to work as a primary school teacher in his original production brigade (village). Because of his brother's "bad" status, Deng was dismissed from this post after a few months and was assigned to labour as an ordinary peasant in the production brigade.

In 1970, in order to implement the "one-strike three-anti" campaign, the brigade cadres examined the background of every member of the brigade and, although there were some previously labelled as "bad elements", it was found that their cases did not meet the standards of the campaign to look for "counter-revolutionaries according to present activities". On the other hand, when Deng's case was examined, the Party Secretary felt that the contrast between Deng's past privileged position and his present one might have made him discontented. This, and the fact that his brother was a "bad element", was the starting point of a long investigation into his past behaviour and activities. The cadres apparently had no other more precise suspicions about Deng; it was because of his background that he was chosen as the main "target" of the campaign in the brigade. The campaign then followed a classical pattern: the cadres mobilized the population to denounce the suspect, and after several weeks they found several witnesses to testify that Deng had spread stories "slandering Chairman Mao" in the past. He was later sentenced to 15 years' imprisonment on this charge. The review *Huang He* suggests that the charges were false and that the main witnesses had been intimidated into testifying.[27] In any event, the reason why Deng was made the object of investigation in the first place was, reportedly, his background.

Since 1949, people having a "bad" class or political background have been more liable than others to political repression. A Canadian journalist, Ross Munro, reported in the *New York Times* of 13 October 1977 that discrimination on the basis of class origin survived in the Chinese countryside in 1977 and somehow still affected the children of people who had long ago been labelled as "class enemies". As has been seen earlier, the authorities acknowledged this problem in an article in the *People's Daily* of 18 February 1978, which stressed that it had always been Party policy to distinguish between children and their parents' wrongdoings. The paper blamed purged leaders for persecuting and slanderously "labelling" the children of people in disgrace. However, this article indicates that the actual practice of using "class labels" has not been abandoned.

The range of political offences

The distinction between criminal and political offences is not clearly drawn by law in China, as all cases are treated in the light of political considerations. For instance, petty offenders who have committed minor theft or engaged in speculation may be merely criticized if they have good political and work records, and good class backgrounds, and if they are not recidivists. On the other hand, the same offence might be punished severely if the offender's social and political background is "bad", in which case his or her "crimes" will be considered to be of a political nature.

On the basis of official accusations against people arrested on political grounds, political offenders can be divided into three main categories:

1. "Historical counter-revolutionaries" (*lishi fangeming*), which is generally the designation for people punished for their activities or position before 1949. This category includes people who are officially regarded as having participated in organized opposition to the CCP before 1949, that is, members of former political parties or organizations opposed to the CCP, former Guomindang intelligence agents, etc., as well as members of the former privileged classes. The majority of offenders in this category were dealt with in the 1950s. However, it is reported that people were still being arrested as "historical counter-revolutionaries" during and after the Cultural Revolution, either because their past histories has been unknown until then and were suddenly discolsed, or else because they were accused of new offences (committed after 1949) for which their cases were reopened and judged in the light of their past.

2. "Active counter-revolutionaries" (*xianxing fangeming*). This term can also be translated as "current counter-revolutionaries": *xianxing* literally means "current activities" or "caught in the act". It is used to designate people accused of involvement in "current" opposition activities, who have no personal record allowing them to be classified as "historical counter-revolutionaries". This label in fact covers a wide range of offences, from simple public expression of dissent to politically motivated common-law offences. It applies, for instance, to people charged with "spreading counter-revolutionary propaganda" (which can be anything opposed to official policy); forming "counter-revolutionary groups" or "cliques" (people who gather for discussions or for planning concerted political action); "sabotage" (destruction of public property or actions related to the economy which are contrary to official policy); "espionage", etc.

3. The third category might be called simply dissenters. It is composed of people who occasionally voice opinions critical of official policy: for instance, the "rightists" (*youpai*); people accused of "spreading reactionary ideas" (*fandong yanlun*); of belonging to a "reactionary small group" (*fandong xiaojituan*); people found guilty of "wild talk" (*guaihua*)—that is, those who have been outspoken in their comments about official policy or the authorities. This category includes also people arrested for having "illicit relations" with foreign countries—which may simply amount to maintaining correspondence with friends or relatives abroad—or listening to "enemy" (foreign) radio broadcasts.

A more precise idea of the range of political offences can be gained from arrests during political campaigns. A review of such campaigns shows that the concept of political offence has varied with the fluctuations of official policy.

People arrested during the early 1950s campaigns of suppression of counter-revolution belong for the most part to the "historical counter-revolutionaries" category. Some of them were, in fact, convicted on criminal charges: murder or looting committed during the civil war or immediately after the change of government, direct or indirect responsibility for war crimes, etc. However, others were detained merely for their political affiliation or social position before 1949—particularly members of the political parties and associations banned by the new authorities, including the Guomindang and its affiliated organizations, the Chinese "secret societies", some religious associations and, on the left, Trotskyist groups. It has been reported that about 200 Trotskyists and sympathizers were arrested between the end of 1952 and the beginning of 1953, most of whom were never heard of again.[28] Among them was Zheng Chaolin, a political theorist and linguist, who joined the CCP in the early 1920s and was expelled from it as a Trotskyist in 1929. He then became active in the Chinese Trotskyist movement and was arrested by the Guomindang in 1931. After his release, seven years later, he pursued his political work and historical studies, while translating Marxist works into Chinese. He stayed in China when the People's Republic was established in 1949 and was arrested in Shanghai in 1952, reportedly for refusing to compromise with the CCP. Little has been heard about him since. However, he was said to be still detained in Shanghai in 1974.[29] If alive, he is now about 78 years old.

Several purification campaigns followed the 1951/52 movement of "suppression of counter-revolution". In 1955 another national campaign against counter-revolutionaries was developed, centering on the case of a writer, Hu Feng, who was cited as an example to the whole country of a new type of counter-revolutionary.

Hu Feng, a poet and literary theorist, born in 1903, had belonged to the ranks of "progressive" writers before 1949. After the establishment of the new government, he became one of the directors of *People's Literature*, an official literary journal, and a member of the National People's Congress. However, while still supporting the new régime overall, he soon started criticizing the rigid standards imposed on literary creation by the Party's literary authorities. In July 1954, he presented a report to the Party Central Committee, expounding his views on this and making recommendations, including a demand for more free debates in literary and artistic circles. Over the next few months, members of the official Chinese Writers' Union attacked his ideas at a series of meetings convened for the purpose. Hu Feng consequently made a self-criticism in January 1955.

It was not, however, judged to be sufficient, as part of it showed that Hu Feng still had "subjective" views. In the spring of 1955, a campaign against him started in the *People's Daily*, which tried to discredit him by publishing extracts from his private correspondence over the previous 10 years. The press campaign mounted against him lasted for weeks and it was soon suggested that he had not simply committed ideological errors but that he was also the leader of a "counter-revolutionary clique". At the end of May 1955, Hu Feng was dismissed from all his posts and later accused of having formed a "conspiratorial group with Guomindang agents". This accusation was based merely on the fact that Hu Feng had gathered around him a group of intellectuals, which was no more than a small literary group. He is reported to have been tried in July 1955. No details of the trial were ever made public. Conflicting reports circulated in June and July 1957 about his imprisonment, some suggesting that he had been released during the "Hundred Flowers" movement (May 1957), others stating that he was still imprisoned.[30] During the Cultural Revolution, Red Guards are reported to have criticized his treatment in prison as being better than average. This seems to be the most recent information about Hu Feng's imprisonment. He would now be 75 years old. If alive, he is likely still to be restricted in one way or another.

Recently, according to a radio broadcast,[31] a provincial newspaper spoke of his case as the "Hu Feng counter-revolutionary clique", in connection with the need to study Chairman Mao's articles on various counter-revolutionary groups.[32] About twenty people, friends or followers of Hu Feng, most of whom were Party members, were accused of belonging to the "Hu Feng clique".

At the same time, another campaign against counter-revolutionaries was launched in June 1955, aimed primarily at certain government departments, the surviving democratic parties[33] and the Communist Party itself, as well as at cultural, industrial and religious circles. Several Chinese religious leaders are known to have been arrested in the course of it.[34]

There are believed to have been rather fewer arrests during this campaign than during those of the early 1950s, when an enormous number were arrested. This was mainly because the 1955 campaign was directed at specific groups, not the majority of the population. Nevertheless, its scope was very broad, and, together with the Hu Feng case, it deeply antagonized intellectuals. Two years later, when they were officially encouraged to speak up during this campaign, some of them argued that an injustice had been done.

The "Hundred Flowers" movement was launched on the initiative of Chairman Mao, with the slogan "Let a Hundred Flowers Blossom, Let a Hundred Schools of Thought Contend". It was an attempt to secure more active participation by the intelligentsia in economic and political affairs and was seen by them as an encouragement to express their opinions on Party policy. When the movement was launched, the Party apparently did not expect that the fundamental principles of its policy would be questioned. This, however, is what happened from May until mid June 1957, when the movement was abruptly halted. For a few weeks, journalists, writers, students, lawyers, members of the remaining "democratic parties" and others strongly criticized the Party's bureaucratic practices and its repression of any potential opposition.

One of the most outspoken critics, a professor from Hankou (Hankow), wrote in a 10,000-word letter to Chairman Mao:

". . . Again, our Constitution provides that 'freedom of the person of citizens is inviolable'. During the campaign for the suppression of counter-revolutionaries in 1955, an untold number of citizens throughout the country were detained by the units where they were working (this did not happen to myself). A great many of them died because they could not endure the struggle. No matter how strong the 'reasons' were for detaining these citizens to conduct struggles against them, this was, after all, a serious violation of human rights . . ."

"We have applied to intellectuals methods of punishment which peasants would not apply to landlords and workers would not apply to capitalists. During the social reform campaigns, unable to endure the spiritual torture and humiliation imposed by the struggle . . . intellectuals who chose to die by jumping from tall buildings, drowning in rivers, swallowing poison, cutting their throats or by other methods, were innumerable . . ."[35]

When the official press started in turn counter-attacking the critics, this letter was published in a regional newspaper as one example of the "vicious attacks" made by the "rightists" against the Party. Many writers, journalists, teachers and students were singled out as scapegoats for the "anti-rightist" campaign which was then launched against this new category of "enemies". Intellectuals constituted the majority of those labelled "rightists", as they had been the most articulate critics.

The "rightists" were treated with varying degrees of "severity" or "leniency". Some of them repudiated their ideas and were allowed to remain at their posts after making, in public, thorough self-criticisms. The majority was probably sent to "rehabilitation" farms; a law adopted for this purpose on 1 August 1957 included provisions applying specifically to the "rightists".[36] "Rehabilitation" was not regarded officially as a criminal punishment (see pp. 80-83) but as a "coercive measure" for the ideological remoulding through labour of rightists and petty offenders.

Some rightists were formally sentenced to terms of imprisonment or of labour-reform. Among them was a 20-year-old girl named Lin Xiling,[37] a student and Party member, who was one of the leaders of the student movement at China People's University in Peking. She is reported to have been sentenced to 20 years of reform through labour with deprivation of civil rights for life and is believed to be still detained.

After the campaign against the rightists, other mass mobilization movements—in particular the "Socialist Education" campaign and the "Four Clean-ups" campaign in 1964-65[38] —led to political arrests until the start of the Cultural Revolution in 1966. However, the anti-rightist campaign can be regarded as the main wave of repression of non-violent and articulate opposition during the period preceding the Cultural Revolution.

Another wave of repression accompanied and followed the Cultural Revolution, but in a totally different context, however, as it occurred in a period of violence and chaos. During the Cultural Revolution itself (1966-68), the judiciary was unable to function or exercise any control. The local Party Committees and the administration—people's councils and administrative committees—were themselves partly dismantled. Consequently, many people were arbitrarily arrested on political grounds, maltreated or even killed by *ad hoc* groups or factions operating on their own. Many examples have been given recently by the official press and radio which blame the "gang of four's followers" for such malpractices. The vice-chairman of the inspection office of Luta Municipal People's Committee (Liaoning province), for instance, is alleged to have been "beaten to death by the gang of four's sinister followers on 7 June 1968 at the age of 63".[39]

At the beginning of the Cultural Revolution (1966), a "Central Cultural Revolution Group" composed of CCP Politburo members was formed in Peking—on the initiative of Chairman Mao—to carry out the Cultural Revolution. Under its instructions, "mass organizations" (Red Guards and other groups) were created in all institutions and encouraged to "attack" those who clung to old habits and ideas [40] and all cadres in the Party and administration who followed a "revisionist" line. Soon, however, some local leaders opposed to the Maoist faction organized their own groups of Red Guards and clashes occurred between rival factions.

The whole Cultural Revolution was marked by a revival of the "class struggle" in an acute form. "Class enemies" were given a new designation: they were branded as "freaks and demons" (*niugui sheshen*). Many people were arbitrarily arrested by one faction or another and detained, sometimes for long periods and without any legal process, in improvised detention places (called *niu lan*—"cow-sheds").

At the same time, the CCP Central Committee and the State Council issued new regulations on counter-revolutionaries which were apparently intended as internal regulations to guide the work of the Public Security (police) and were not published. They were issued in January 1967 and stipulated that the following acts were "counter-revolutionary" and should be punished according to law:

– sending counter-revolutionary anonymous letters;
– posting or distributing secretly or openly counter-revolutionary handbills;
– writing or shouting reactionary slogans;
– attacking or vilifying Chairman Mao and Vice-Chairman Lin Biao. [41]

This last is particularly important. It is reported to have been applied as an article of law until 1971 and has been identified as "Clause No. 6" of the Public Security regulations (*gongan liujiao*). Many people were arrested under this clause which specified that those who said or wrote (*yan lun*) anything "attacking" (*gongji*) Chairman Mao or Vice-Chairman Lin Biao were "active counter-revolutionaries". It was used later during the campaigns which succeeded the Cultural Revolution.

From 1967 to 1968 the conflicts between rival factions degenerated into armed struggles in many places. The army units sent to restore order sometimes took sides. Some of them, in co-operation with the "winning" civilian factions, carried out large-scale arrests and, in some places, massacres occurred. This was apparently against official instructions. As early as April 1967, the Central Military Commission issued an Order prohibiting "arbitrary arrests", "particularly large-scale arrests", and stipulating that "counter-revolutionary elements" should be arrested when "conclusive evidence had been found" and that such arrests should first be "approved". [42]

As the Cultural Revolution was marked by widespread factional violence, it is likely that a number of those arrested in 1968 had used or advocated violence. However, there was encouragement for violence from people at a very high level—by some members of the "Central Cultural Revolution Group" who advocated seizure of power from the old establishment and were later purged for "ultra-leftist" tendencies. The early official slogans of the Cultural Revolution were also along these lines. In addition, the massive arrests of 1967 to 1968 seem to have been made at random, according to local alliances or antagonisms, and members of the "winning" factions who were themselves responsible for violence took advantage of the army intervention to retaliate against their opponents.

Although there were, therefore, "unauthorized" arrests, the central authorities themselves took strong measures to eliminate opposition. Towards the end of 1968, a national campaign to "clean up the class ranks" (*qingli jieji duiwu*) was launched by the CCP Central Committee, partly to restore order after the chaos of the Cultural Revolution and partly to identify those who were in disagreement with official policy. As with all new campaigns, an official document issued by the CCP Central Committee was sent to the local branches of the Party and of the Public Security who are in charge of implementing the specific instructions of the movement. This campaign was particularly aimed at conducting a very thorough investigation of the cadres' political background, but it affected a far larger range of people. The "targets" of the "clean the class ranks" campaign are reported to have been the following categories of people:

— those who had "attacked" Chairman Mao;
— those who had "attacked" Vice-Chairman Lin Biao;
— those who acted as "black hands" during the Cultural Revolution (this refers to cadres who were not directly involved in the Cultural Revolution struggle and remained "deliberately in the background" in order to "manipulate" other people, gain favours or protection);
— those who had caused the destruction of equipment, food, buildings, etc., or the deaths of people during the Cultural Revolution;
— those among the "five bad elements" who had not reformed properly;
— those cadres who had been downgraded or dismissed during the 1964 "four clean-ups" campaign.

The central authorities were apparently aware that abuses could occur in the course of the movement and an additional directive from Chairman Mao was officially issued in December 1968 to guide the "cleaning of the class ranks". Its purpose was to prevent the labelling of too many people as counter-revolutionaries:

"In purifying our class ranks, it is necessary to take a firm hold first and then pay attention to the policy. In treating the counter-revolutionary elements and those who have made mistakes, it is necessary to pay attention to the policy. The target of attack must be narrowed and more people must be helped through education. Evidence, investigation, and study should be stressed. It is strictly forbidden to extort confessions and accept such confessions. As for good people who have made mistakes, we must give them more help through education. When they are awakened, we must liberate them without delay."[43]

The "cleaning of the class ranks" was closely followed in 1969 by a "loyalty" campaign (*chongzi yundong*), said to have been initiated by Lin Biao as a test of everyone's loyalty to Chairman Mao and to his successor—Lin Biao himself. In 1970, the "one-strike three-anti" campaign (*yida sanfan*) was launched, reportedly on the initiative of Chairman Mao.[44] It was aimed both at political offenders and at people who had committed "economic" offences (speculation, black-marketeering, corruption). It resulted in numerous arrests and executions and is reported to have been the most severe purification campaign since the 1950s.

A considerable number of people are said to have been either temporarily detained or sentenced from the end of the Cultural Revolution until the early 1970s. Many were political offenders. A wall poster displayed in the streets of Canton in 1974 stated: ". . . in Guangdong province alone nearly 40,000 revolutionary masses and cadres were massacred and more than a million revolutionary cadres and masses were imprisoned, put under control and struggled against."[45]

Practically no attention was paid to normal legal procedures during that period. Innocent people were therefore detained without charge for months or years and others were sentenced on totally arbitrary grounds. Some examples are given below.

At the end of the Cultural Revolution, Wang was a young high-school graduate working in the production brigade of a people's commune in Guangdong province—like many other young people who are sent to work in the countryside after graduation. According to one of his friends, who has now left China, Wang was arrested in 1968 after a "counter-revolutionary" slogan was discovered painted on a wall in his production brigade (village). Wang was reportedly singled out from among the suspects because he had a "bad" class origin and was not on very good terms with the peasants in the brigade. During a search, his diary was found and what he had written was taken as evidence that he was somehow "dissatisfied with the Party". On this basis and without further evidence that he was the author of the slogan, Wang was sentenced to 10 years of reform through labour and sent to a labour camp in the province. After Lin Biao fell from power in 1971, the judge who had sentenced Wang was dismissed and Wang's family appealed for a review of his case. After a long re-investigation, Wang was finally released in 1974. However, he had by that time spent six years in prison and was so shocked by his experience that he is said to have shown signs of mental instability after his release.

The testimony below is that of a young man who told Amnesty International how he spent two years in a detention center without being formally charged with any particular offence. In 1970, Zhang was an "educated youth"—that is, a high-school graduate from the city who had been sent to work in the countryside at the end of the Cultural Revolution. While he was still in the city, Zhang and some friends had formed a group to discuss political theory and study the works of Marx and Lenin. This was not unusual in the period 1967-68 as many young people were trying to understand the change of policy which marked the end of the Cultural Revolution. After being sent to the country, Zhang kept in touch with his friends. In May 1970 he was arrested in the rural production brigade where he worked and accused of belonging to a "clique" (*jituan*)—the Chinese word implies illegal activities. His arrest had been prompted by the accidental interception of a letter addressed to him, in which a friend advised him, among other things, to read more articles by Marx and Lenin and not to "involve himself in any trouble" now that the situation was very tense (the "one-strike three-anti" campaign was still going on). Zhang was questioned about his friends and the study group to which he belonged, and pressed to write down what they had discussed. After two weeks, as he had not confessed to any "crime", he was sent to the county detention center "to reflect" on his faults. Questioning continued there and it became obvious to Zhang that his friends were also being investigated. His interrogators were trying to find out whether the group had said anything critical of Mao or of official policy. Zhang never confessed to anything other than what the group had been discussing: Marxist-Leninist theory. He was finally released after two years without having been formally charged. He believed that his release in May 1972 was due to the reviewing of cases which started after the purge of Lin Biao. However, he was given no official explanation. He was told only that he was released "in accordance with the policy towards educated youths", which was a "lenient policy".

According to another account from a refugee, in 1970 a small-scale campaign was launched in Guangdong province against people who had "illicit relations" with foreign countries (*gou lian*) and "committed sabotage from the inside" (*ce fan*)—in other words, people accused of espionage. Having such "illicit relations" can also, however, mean anything from listening to foreign radio broadcasts to corresponding with friends or relatives abroad. The search for spies is more intense in Guangdong province than in other regions, due to the constant passage of travellers to or from Hong Kong. It is reported that during this campaign, the police of a people's commune named *hou jie*, in Dongguang county, suspected a resident of Hong Kong, who was on a visit to the commune, of being a spy. The man was arrested, questioned at length about his "work and accomplices" and threatened with being prevented from returning to Hong Kong if he did not confess. According to official policy, "confession and sincere repentance" are generally rewarded by "lenient" treatment. Frightened at the prospect of otherwise being given a long sentence and of being prevented indefinitely from returning to Hong Kong, the man admitted that he was a spy and gave the names of people whom he alleged to be working with him. They were arrested, questioned in a similar fashion and in turn gave names of others involved. More people were therefore arrested. At that point, however, the police wondered from what source such a large ring of spies was financed. The money was unlikely to have come from abroad, as it was difficult to smuggle in large sums unnoticed. Surmising that it could only have come from neighbouring communes in the county itself, the police then investigated the financial officers of various communes, and several who had not carried out their work well in the past were also arrested. The affair lasted for about a year, assuming enormous proportions, and was finally dropped as no real evidence could be discovered about the "spy ring". All those who had been arrested were then released. However, harsh pressure, including beating, was reported to have been used in the course of investigation, and some people, unable to bear the pressure, are said to have committed suicide.

After the disappearance of Lin Biao in September 1971, several political campaigns succeeded each other without interruption until 1976. They reflected increasing conflict amongst the leadership, which resulted, shortly after Mao's death in September 1976, in the purge and arrest of four "radical" leaders[46] now stigmatized in the official press as the "gang of four".

From 1972-73 onwards, efforts were made to review the cases of people arbitrarily sentenced or detained on political grounds, when a movement of "rectification to criticize Lin Biao" (*Pi Lin zhengfeng*) was launched, and releases occurred. However, the process of review seems to have been impeded by other campaigns sponsored by the "radical" leaders.[47] The official Chinese press has since given many examples of people arrested on political grounds during that period.

One well-known case reported in the *People's Daily* on 9 December 1977 is the "incident of the Machenfu Commune Middle-school" in Henan province. In July 1973, a student at the school committed suicide after being criticized by a responsible member of the school, Luo Changji, and a teacher, Yang Tiancheng, for failing an English examination and arguing that she did not need to study a foreign language. A regional investigation was conducted, but was reportedly taken over in 1974 by two special envoys of the "gang of four" who turned it into a political affair. Consequently Luo Changji and Yang Tiancheng were arrested and sent to prison as counter-revolutionaries. According to the *People's Daily*, the Henan Provincial Party Committee recently decided to "reverse the verdicts" passed on Luo and Yang, which suggests that they have been released.

Other cases have been officially reported, in particular those of artists and writers arbitrarily detained or harassed[48] and of cadres "persecuted" by the "gang of four".[49] While such rehabilitations— and some liberalization in the cultural and economic field—are now taking place, people accused of having been "followers" of the "gang of four" have come under attack.

A national campaign to criticize the "gang of four" was launched at the end of 1976 and was still going on in early 1978. Official accounts of the campaign show that a large number of regional or local cadres are being purged or arrested. Some of them have been accused of violent acts or unlawful use of power which resulted in the persecution of other people. However, others have been accused simply of political "manoeuvring". Furthermore, the constant directives by the official media on how to carry out the campaign show that anyone suspected of the slightest sympathy with the ideology of the "gang of four" must be "thoroughly investigated".

A radio broadcast on 14 October 1977 from Huhehaote, the capital of Inner Mongolia, was reported to have stressed that the following distinctions should be made in the work of investigation: "strictly distinguish between those who said something wrong under the gang's influence and the backbone elements who were privy to the gang's conspiracy; and even among the backbone elements, strictly distinguish between those who, since October 1976,[50] have expressed their willingness to repent and make amends, exposed the gang's crimes and broken with them, and the diehards who continue to put up an obstinate fight" [51] This is a classic reminder of official policy towards offenders: those who simply made "mistakes" and show that they are ready to mend their ways may be allowed to go free after some criticism or mildly punished, whereas those accused of committing "crimes" are formally sentenced, but with varying degrees of severity depending on how thoroughly they "admit their guilt".

Official sources show that the current investigation concerns a large number of people, but apart from some major "culprits" whose cases have been made exemplary, they rarely mention names. However, some arrests have been reported by other sources. In Canton five members of the Standing Committee of the Guangdong Provincial Revolutionary Committee were reported to have been purged in 1977 and three of them are said to be detained for investigation into their connections with Wang Hungwen (one member of the "gang of four").[52] The five are all former Red Guards now in their thirties who were appointed to the Revolutionary Committee in 1968 as a result of the compromises worked out at the end of the Cultural Revolution. The three reported to be detained are Liu Junyi, Tian Huagui and Liang Qintang. Liu Junyi had been actively involved in the Guangdong Provincial Workers' Congress and the Canton Municipal Committee of the Chinese Communist Youth League. Together with Tian Huagui, he had been elected a full member of the CCP Central Committee in 1969 and Liang Qintang was elected an alternate member.

Unrelated to the campaign against the "gang of four", some cases of offenders sentenced on political grounds were also reported in 1977. Among them were the three authors of a wall poster displayed in Canton in 1974 who were put "under surveillance" in 1975 after their poster was criticized. They were later reported to have been labelled "counter-revolutionary" and sent to labour camps. According to an unconfirmed report, the leader of the group, Li Zhengtian, was sentenced to life imprisonment in 1977.[53]

Court notices are posted in public periodically to announce, some time after judgment, the sentences passed on various offenders. Such notices were seen by travellers to various cities in 1977, who said that they were about both criminal and political offenders. One court notice which appeared in Shenyang (Liaoning province) in early 1977 mentioned the case of a "professional rightist" sentenced to 20 years' imprisonment for his "counter-revolutionary" views. The

man, aged 61, was not named. According to the notice, he had previously been sentenced twice, once for corruption: "He fabricated
and spread counter-revolutionary rumours . . . wrote numerous
letters in which he attacked the Chinese Communist Party and went
so far as to blame Chairman Mao. In his notebook he had written
down counter-revolutionary poems and slogans which covered more
than 10,000 characters [words]. He is a reactionary who has
dedicated himself to the cause of the Guomindang and the sworn
enemy of our socialist system."[54]

Another court notice posted in Nanjing (Jiangsu province) in April
1977 also included a number of political cases. According to the
translation published in the German magazine *Der Spiegel* of 22
August 1977, the notice gave the following information about the
case of a "counter-revolutionary": "The counter-revolutionary Liu
Yongda, male, 32 years old, from Jiangsu province, was in Prison
No. 1 of Jiangsu where he had been sent for reform through labour",
before the last review of his case in 1977.

Liu had first been given the "cap" (label) of "bad element" in
1966 for "misbehaving with a young girl" and "spreading reactionary
talk" and consequently he had to work under supervision. "In 1969
he wrote reactionary slogans" and was given a five-year sentence "to
be served under the supervision of the masses" (this probably means
"control", as five years is unusually long for simple "supervision").
"In 1971 he again wrote reactionary slogans and his sentence was
increased by five years." The notice goes on to say that during the
time of reform through labour (Liu was probably sent to a labour
camp, or possibly to the Prison No. 1 of Jiangsu province mentioned
above), "the criminal Liu again wrote reactionary slogans and
announced reactionary solutions", for which he was sentenced to
death with suspension of execution for two years. According to the
court notice, "The criminal Liu however was obstinate in his counter-
revolutionary attitude; on 19 September 1976 he again pronounced
counter-revolutionary slogans and his attacks were aimed directly at
our great leader, Chairman Mao." The notice stated that "facts show
that his crimes were considerable" and that "the court in accordance
with the law imposed the death sentence on the counter-revolutionary
Liu, which is to be carried out on the spot."

"On 1 April 1977 the court had the criminal Liu taken bound to
the place of execution, where he was shot."

The scope of political imprisonment

Due to the scarcity of information and the fact that official statistics

江苏省南京市中级人民法院

布　告

在英明领袖华主席为首的党中央的领导下，全市人民高举毛主席的伟大旗帜，坚决贯彻华主席抓纲治国的战略决策，深入揭批"四人帮"的滔天罪行，抓革命，促生产，促工作，促战备，形势一片大好。但是，失败的阶级还要挣扎，一小撮阶级敌人总是千方百计地进行破坏和捣乱，为了保卫伟大领袖和导师毛主席，保卫华主席，党中央，保卫毛主席的革命路线，保卫揭批"四人帮"的伟大斗争，保卫"工业学大庆"、"农业学大寨"的伟大群众运动，保护人民生命财产安全，维护社会主义秩序，进一步巩固和加强无产阶级专政，本院依法判处现行反革命分子张文秀等十三名罪犯，现公布于下：

反革命犯　亚××
反革命犯　冯××
强好杀人犯　×××

反革命犯　许忠魁
同案犯　金跃
强好犯　彭国祥
行凶抢劫犯　谢世勇
同案犯　朱茂军

流氓犯　胡廷昇
扒路强奸犯　端木毅
打砸抢犯　斗方宝

诈骗犯　刘然
投机倒把犯　张元镇

全市人民要最紧密地团结在以华主席为首的党中央周围，牢记党的基本路线，千万不要忘记阶级斗争，保持高度革命警惕，坚决打击一小撮阶级敌人的破坏活动。党的政策历来是"坦白从宽，抗拒从严"，我们严正警告一小撮阶级敌人，只有停止作恶，坦白交待，争取从宽处理，才是唯一出路。如若执迷不悟，继续作恶，负隅顽抗，必将受到无产阶级专政的严厉制裁。

一九七七年四月一日

（供内部宣读、张贴）

Public notice from Nanjing's Intermediate People's Court, Jiangsu province, announcing sentences passed on 13 offenders, three of whom were sentenced to death with immediate execution, including the "counter-revolutionary" Liu Yongda. The notice is dated 1 April 1977.

are not available, the number of prisoners of conscience in China cannot be estimated.

A few figures are given below about "counter-revolutionaries" sentenced during the first decade of the PRC. However, these must be examined with care, especially since they do not distinguish between those offenders held on purely political grounds and those charged with common-law offences, although the latter were labelled "counter-revolutionary" because such offences had, or were seen officially as having, a political purpose. (It must be pointed out however that [common-law] "ordinary" crimes in China include some "economic" offences or offences related to social behaviour which would not be prosecuted under criminal law or even regarded as offences in other societies.)

These figures all refer to the first decade of the PRC and cannot be taken as a basis for assessing the number of prisoners of conscience held at present. Apart from people who are under some form of temporary restriction, the prisoner population itself may have varied substantially over the years because of political upheavals. In the past 10 years, the apparent quick succession, or sometimes the simultaneity, of releases and arrests make it particularly difficult to present any reliable estimates.

The figures given below are all based on official or unofficial Chinese sources. A comparison shows important differences between some of them.

According to documents collected and circulated by Red Guards during the Cultural Revolution, Chairman Mao said in April 1956 at an enlarged meeting of the Party Politburo that "two to three million counter-revolutionaries had been executed, imprisoned or placed under control in the past".[55]

The same collection of documents includes another unpublished text of Mao's giving figures for the 1955 campaign against counter-revolutionaries.[56] According to this text, from the beginning of the campaign in (June) 1955 up till December 1956, more than four million individuals were investigated, revealing 160,000 "doubtful elements". Of the latter, 38,000 people—none of whom was executed—were detained as counter-revolutionaries and over 120,000 were declared innocent and presented with excuses. The text has an optimistic tone, as at the end of 1956 Mao was preparing to launch the "Hundred Flowers" liberalization movement. He stressed that only a small number of counter-revolutionaries were arrested during the preceding year and that they were treated mildly—38,000 is indeed a low figure compared with estimates of arrests for the previous years.

Edgar Snow also mentions in his book *Red China Today*[57] the figure given by Zhou Enlai (Chou En-lai) of 830,000 "enemies" of the people "destroyed" up till 1954. Edgar Snow remarks that "destroy" does not necessarily mean "execute". According to Polish sources, the original unpublished version of Mao's speech "On the Correct Handling of Contradictions Among the People" gave an estimate of 800,000 executions up till 1954.[58]

In June 1957 Zhou Enlai presented a report to the National People's Congress[59] in which he gave the following breakdown of counter-revolutionaries' cases: 16.8% had been sentenced to death, most of them between 1949 and 1952; 42.3% had been sentenced to terms of reform-through-labour, of whom 16.7% were still detained in 1957; 32% had been put under control, of whom 9.1% were still under control in 1957; 8.9% "benefited from measures of clemency" and were released after "a period of re-education" (probably without being sentenced). Zhou Enlai specified that 48.5% of those sentenced to reform-through-labour or put under control in the previous years had been released by 1957.

In 1954 there was another indication of the number of people deprived of their political rights. In the 1954 elections to the National People's Congress nearly 10,000,000 "still unrehabilitated class enemies"[60] were not allowed to vote. This figure does not refer only to people detained or put under control but includes other categories of people deprived of their rights without necessarily being affected by other penalties.[61]

According to the texts collected by Red Guards, Chairman Mao said in May 1958 that, after December 1957, "still one hundred thousand rightists came to light among primary school teachers, counting for a third of the rightists in the whole country".[62] "To let them free or not is a policy question . . . Among primary school teachers there are many rightists, a hundred thousand among the three hundred thousand rightists. The opposition of three hundred thousand rightists exists. To release them to teach six hundred million people is in our interest."[63] In another talk in March 1958 Mao also gave the following proportion: "The rightists make up two per cent of the bourgeoisie. The great majority of these can in future be changed and transformed".[64]

Speculations about the number of prisoners have been based also on official statements that "well over ninety-five per cent" of the population "support the socialist system" and should be "united with", and that "less than five per cent " are hostile to the socialist state and should be reformed. Such statements are frequent in Mao's official writings and still appear in today's official press. One of

Mao's unpublished talks includes a precise reference to this percentage: he is reported to have said in April 1958 that "the landlords, rich peasants, counter-revolutionaries, bad elements and rightists . . . altogether represent about five per cent of the population, more or less thirty million. They are the class enemies, who must still be reformed. . . . If one out of ten can be reformed, this will be a success."[65]

However, it should be pointed out that the percentage of "less than five per cent" who "should be reformed" does not refer to the prisoner population (therefore still less to the prisoners held on political grounds). Official texts show that this percentage seems to represent a crude estimate of the maximum number of people who may be investigated for either criminal or political reasons during purification campaigns. Towards the end of these campaigns, directives are repeatedly given (to local authorities) to "narrow the target of attack" and to "strictly distinguish" between those who have merely made "mistakes" and those who have committed "crimes". Normally only the latter are to be formally convicted; consequently, the number of those eventually sentenced may be a small proportion of all those investigated. The "less than five per cent" indicates, nevertheless, that the number of people liable to be investigated and temporarily detained on criminal or political grounds during purification campaigns may be very large in proportion to the adult population of China.

Many references to these percentages were made in the official press in the course of the campaign against the "gang of four". According to a radio broadcast, the *Xinjiang Daily*, for instance, stated on 18 October 1977: "With the deepening of the movement, more attention must be paid to policy. . . . In conducting investigations, it is essential to . . . unite with over ninety-five per cent of the cadres and masses and achieve maximum isolation of the most die-hard elements and concentrate our blows at them. In the meantime, it is necessary to deal telling blows at those imperialist rich peasants, counter-revolutionaries, bad elements and rightists who hate socialism . . ."[66]

An estimate of the proportion of "diehards who are absolutely opposed to socialism" given by Mao in 1957 was quoted recently in an article by Chairman Hua Guofeng when the fifth volume of Mao's *Selected Works* was published:

"Basing himself on the experience of the anti-rightist struggle in 1957, Chairman Mao pointed out that the people who favour socialism account for ninety per cent of the total population of the country while those who do not favour or oppose socialism make up ten per cent, of whom eight out of ten may be won over through work so that the people who favour socialism may reach ninety-eight per cent, and the diehards who are absolutely opposed to socialism make up only two per cent."[67]

32

Notes

1 Edgar Snow, *Red China Today, the Other Side of the River*, Penguin Books, London, 1976, pp. 357-359.

2 Various translations of the main legal documents of the PRC are available, in particular in Albert Blaustein, *Fundamental Legal Documents of Communist China*, New Jersey, 1962; Jerome Alan Cohen, *The Criminal Process in the People's Republic of China, 1949-1963, An Introduction*, Harvard University Press, Cambridge, Mass., 1968; Tsien Tche-hao, *La République populaire de Chine, Droit constitutionel et Institution*, Librairie Générale de Droit et de Jurisprudence, Paris, 1970. Some laws have been published also in translation in Peking by Foreign Languages Press. Unless otherwise specified, the translation followed in this report is that of Jerome A. Cohen.

3 Quotations from the Constitution hereafter are from the English translation given by the New China News Agency on 7 March 1978.

4 See "One must strengthen the Revolutionary Legal System", an article by the Theoretical group of Shanghai High People's Court in the *People's Daily* of 15 July 1977.

5 Approved by the Government Administration Council on 27 June 1952, promulgated by the Ministry of Public Security on 17 July 1952; see Cohen, op. cit., 277-279.

6 Chapter III, p. 84.

7 Chapter III, p. 84.

8 Mao said in 1957: "In the course of cleaning out counter-revolutionaries good people were sometimes mistaken for bad, and such things still happen today." (*Selected Works of Mao Tsetung*, Vol. V, Peking, 1977, p.392.)

9 "Circumstances and opinions concerning the present struggle for the suppression of counter-revolutionaries", *People's Daily* of 24 June 1956, translated in the review *Saturne*, No. 8, June-July 1956, pp.59-68.

10 This speech, entitled "On the Ten Major Relationships", was made at an enlarged meeting of the Party Politburo on 25 April 1956. One part deals with "The Relationship Between Revolution and Counter-Revolution": see *Selected Works of Mao Tsetung*, Vol. V, pp. 298-301.

11 According to unpublished documents gathered by Red Guards during the Cultural Revolution, another address to the Politburo made by Mao earlier in April 1956 revealed that two to three million counter-revolutionaries had been "killed, imprisoned or placed under control" in the previous years. See p. 28.

12 Mao said: "For instance, they kill cattle, set fire to granaries, wreck factories, steal information and put up reactionary posters."

13 "On the People's Democratic Dictatorship", *Selected Works of Mao Tsetung*, Vol. IV, Peking, 1969, pp. 411-24. Quotations hereafter are from this edition.

14 "The contradiction between the working class and the bourgeoisie is the principal contradiction in China", 6 June 1952, *Selected Works of Mao Tsetung*, Vol. V, p. 77.

15 ibid., pp. 384-421.

16 On the "rightists" and the "Hundred Flowers" movement, see p. 17.

17 "Report on the Revision of the Constitution" delivered on 1 March 1978 at the first session of the Fifth National People's Congress by Ye Jianying, New China News Agency in English of 7 March 1978; SWB, FE/5759.

18 "Decisions Concerning the Differentiation of Class Status in the Countryside", adopted by the Government Administration Council on 4 August 1950, in Blaustein, op. cit., pp. 291-324.

19 Blaustein, p. 311-312.

20 ibid., p. 316.

21 *Hsiang:* an administrative division below the level of the county in the countryside; the county is a division of the district which is itself a division of the province. The "county people's government" is the executive body or administration of the county.

22 The "old liberated areas" refers to the areas of central north China which were under the control of the Communist Party prior to 1949.

23 Blaustein, op. cit., p. 324.

24 See *Deviance and Social Control in Chinese Society*, edited by Amy Auerbacher Wilson, Sidney Leonard Greenblatt and Richard Whittingham Wilson, Praeger, New York, 1977, in particular p. 133.

25 The "Case of one counter-revolutionary", *Huang He*, No. 1, 1976. Translated in the reviews *Minus 8*, July-August 1976 and *Esprit*, 7-8, July-August 1977, pp. 66-78.

26 This expression (in Chinese *xianxing fangeming*) can also be translated by "active" or "current counter-revolutionary". In contrast to "historical counter-revolutionaries" (*lishi fangeming*), which designates people considered counter-revolutionaries for their acts or position before 1949, this expression refers to people accused of committing political offences in their "present activities", whatever their class origin and past. See p. 14 for further details.

27 See Appendix 4, p. 158, for detailed information on the way the investigation was conducted.

28 *Revolutionaries in Mao's Prisons, The Case of the Chinese Trotskyists*, by Li Fu-jen and Peng Shu-tse, Pathfinder Press, New York, 1974.

29 See "Teng's comrade still behind bars" an article by Greg Benton in the British newspaper, the *Guardian* of 9 November 1977.

30 *Time* of 24 June 1957 and *New York Times* of 11 June and 19 July 1957, quoted in Merle Goldman, *Literary Dissent in Communist China*, Harvard University Press, Cambridge, Mass., 1967, p. 293.

31 SWB FE/5601 of 30 August 1977, quoting extracts from an article on the criticism of the "gang of four" in the *Tibet Daily* of 19 August 1977.

32 Hu Feng's case is mentioned in Mao's *Selected Works*, Vol. V, pp. 172-183. Numerous details on his case have been published in the official press of the period. See also Goldman, op. cit., in particular pp. 144-157.

33 In 1949, the leaders of some democratic parties were represented at the Chinese People's Political Consultative Conference, a united front including non-communists and overseas Chinese which has survived to this day. However, these parties survive only in name and are not allowed to carry out independent political activities.

34 See Appendix 2, p. 153.

35 Letter from Yang Shih-chan, published by the Hankou (Hankow) *Ch'ang Chiang Daily* of 13 July 1957, translation from Roderick MacFarquhar, *The Hundred Flowers*, Stevens and Sons, London, 1960, pp. 94-95.

36 "Decision of the State Council of the PRC Relating to Problems of Rehabilitation Through Labour", approved 1 August 1957, promulgated 3 August 1957; see Chapter III, p. 80, on this punishment.

37 See Appendix 1, p. 151.

38 On the aims of these campaigns, see *Documents of the Chinese Communist Party Central Committee*, September 1956–April 1969, Vol. I, Union Research Institute, Hong Kong, 1971, pp. 744-748, and pp. 754-757.

39 Broadcast from Luta on 11 December 1977, in SWB FE/5699 of 22 December 1977.

40 A campaign to destroy the "Four Olds" was launched in summer 1966. The "Four Olds" were: old ideas, old customs, old culture, old habits.

41 "Some Regulations of the CCP Central Committee and the State Council concerning the Strengthening of Public Security Work in the Great Proletarian Cultural Revolution", 13 January 1967, in *CCP Documents of the Great Proletarian Cultural Revolution 1966-67*, Union Research Institute, Hong Kong, 1968, pp. 175-177.

42 See "Order of the Central Military Commission", 6 April 1967, in *CCP Documents of the Great Proletarian Cultural Revolution 1966-67*, pp. 409-411.

43 *Mao's Papers–Anthology and Bibliography* by Jerome Chen, Oxford University Press, London, 1970, p. 157. This directive has been quoted again recently in an article in the *People's Daily* of 8 September 1977 to commemorate the first anniversary of Mao's death.

44 See above, p. 12, and Chapter II, p. 45.

45 "On Socialist Democracy and Legal System" by Li Yizhe; various translations of the poster exist, in particular in *"Chinois, si vous saviez . . ."*, Paris, 1976; *Issues and Studies*, January 1976; *"China: Wer gegen wen?"*, Berlin, 1977.

46 They were: Jiang Qing (Mao's widow) and three Politburo members originally from Shanghai–Wang Hungwen, Yao Wenyuan and Zhang Chunqiao.

47 Following the movement of "rectification to criticize Lin Biao", there were between 1973 and 1976 the following campaigns:
   – the "anti-tide" campaign (*fanchaoliu*) whose main slogan was to "dare to go against the tide". It opposed the tendency to revert to practices dating from before the Cultural Revolution, and was sponsored by the "radicals".
   – the "Criticize Confucius" movement (*Pi Kong*), said to have been launched by the "radicals" to attack Zhou Enlai and the "moderate faction" inside the Party. However, the "moderates" transformed this campaign into:
   – the "Criticize Lin Biao, Criticize Confucius" campaign (*Pi Lin Pi Kong*), in which a parallel was drawn between Lin Biao's ideology and that of Confucius.
   – The campaign against "capitalist roaders" or movement of "anti-reversal of the verdicts by the rightists" (*fan youche fanan*). Sponsored by the radicals, it was attacking the rehabilitation of cadres purged during the Cultural Revolution.

48 See article "Now it's China's cultural thaw" by Harrison E. Salisbury in the *New York Times Magazine* of 4 December 1977.

49 See Ian Mackenzie's report from Shanghai for Reuter's of 22 September 1977.

50 The "gang of four" was arrested in October 1976.

51 SWB, FE/5645, 20 October 1977.

52 See in the *Far Eastern Economic Review* of 9 September 1977 an article by Raymond Yao.

53 *Far Eastern Economic Review* of 15 July 1977; see Appendix 5, p. 163. for more details on this case.

54 See *Esprit*, July-August 1977, p. 59 and *Der Spiegel*, No. 35, 22 August 1977, p. 105.

55 *Mao Zidong Sixiang Wansui* (Long Live Mao Tsetung Thought) 1969, pp. 38-39. This collection presents texts of Mao's writings and talks from 1949 to 1968, as gathered by Red Guards. Many of these texts, including the one mentioned here, have not been officially published. They are generally believed to be authentic, but their accuracy is difficult to assess. Some of them are now available in Volume V of Mao Tsetung's *Selected Works* which presents an edited version of the original texts.

56 "Directives given to some representatives of the first session of the Second Congress of the Trade and Industry National Federation", 8 December 1956, *Mao Zidong Sixiang Wansui*, 1969, p. 67; translated in Mao Tse-toung [sic] *Le Grand Livre Rouge*, Paris, 1975, pp. 31-32.

57 Snow, op. cit., p. 346.

58 Mao's talk "On Contradictions" was delivered on 17 February 1957 but was not published until 18 June 1957 in the *People's Daily*. The published version contained modifications of the original. Extracts from the original, according to the "Warsaw version", are given in MacFarquhar, op. cit., pp. 270-271.

59 Published in the *People's Daily* of 26 June 1957, translated in *Saturne* No. 14, August-September 1957, p. 84; extracts also available in SWB, 27 June 1957, p. 1.

60 Figure given in Edgar Snow, op. cit., p. 318.

61 The Electoral Law of 1953 listed as follows those not allowed to vote: (1) Elements of the landlord class whose status has not yet been changed according to law; (2) Counter-revolutionaries who have been deprived of political rights according to law; (3) Others who have been deprived of political rights according to law; (4) Insane persons (Article 5).

62 Talk of 17 May 1958 at the Second Session of the 8th Congress of the CCP, in *Mao Zidong Sixiang Wansui*, 1969, p.207.

63 Talk of 20 May 1958, ibid., p. 215.

64 Talk of 20 March 1958 at the Chengtu Conference, in Stuart Schram, *Mao Tse-tung Unrehearsed*, Penguin Books, Harmondsworth, 1975, p.112.

65 Talk at the Hankou Conference, 6 April 1958, in *Mao Zidong Sixiang Wansui*, 1969, p. 181.

66 "Thoroughly crush the bourgeois factional set-up of the gang of four as well as that of their sinister henchmen in Xinjiang", *Xinjiang Daily* of 18 October 1977, in SWB, FE/5649, 25 October 1977.

67 "Continue the Revolution Under the Dictatorship of the Proletariat to the End", Hua Guofeng's study of the fifth volume of Mao's *Selected Works*, in *Hsinhua Weekly*, English edition, Issue 430, 5 May 1977, p. 7 (translation of NCNA's report from Peking, 30 April 1977).

The Judicial Process

According to the Constitution adopted in March 1978, the cases of offenders who go through a complete judicial process, from arrest to trial, should now involve three "organizations": the Public Security (police), the Procuratorates and the Courts. (Together with the penal establishments, they are officially referred to as the "dictatorship organizations".) The Public Security agencies are in charge of the detention and investigation of offenders. The Procuratorates deal with reinvestigation and review of cases and generally have the task of ensuring that all citizens and institutions observe the law. The Courts deal with trials.

These three institutions also dealt with offenders before 1966. During the Cultural Revolution, however, the local branches of the police and judiciary were partly paralysed and "mass organizations" were created to ensure the maintenance of public order. During the following years, the Procuratorates—which had previously played a role in investigation and review of cases—disappeared and were officially abolished when the Constitution was amended in 1975. The 1975 Constitution specified that their former functions and powers were to be exercised by the organs of the Public Security at various levels (Article 25). In the past ten years, therefore, the two institutions in charge of the arrest, investigation and the trial of offenders have been the Public Security agencies and the Courts.

Parallel with the normal law-enforcement apparatus are other organizations within the administration, the Party and the army. These are internal committees in charge of controlling civil servants, Party members and the military. The case of an offender in one of these categories is generally dealt with by the internal control committee of his or her organization and not by the police and the courts at the corresponding level. In a speech "On the Ten Major Relationships" made on 25 April 1956 at an enlarged meeting of the Party Politburo,[1] Mao Tsetung made particularly clear the approved way to handle "counter-revolutionaries in Party and government organs, schools and army units", as distinct from counter-revolutionaries "in society at large". The text showed that these two categories of political offenders were to be treated differently—as regards both procedure and punishment.

First, Mao said, "in clearing out counter-revolutionaries in Party and government organs, schools and army units, we must adhere to the policy started in Yan'an of killing none and arresting few". "Confirmed counter-revolutionaries" in these official institutions "are to be screened by the organizations concerned", but, unlike counter-revolutionaries "in society at large", "they are not to be arrested by the public security bureaux, prosecuted by the procuratorial organs or tried by the law courts." The great majority of such cases should be handled by the "organizations concerned":

"Well over ninety out of every hundred of these counter-revolutionaries should be dealt with in this way. This is what we mean by arresting few. As for executions, kill none."

Mao explained that civil servants and members of the Party and the army should not be executed because "such executions would yield no advantage". Besides, Mao said, "if you cut off a head by mistake, there is no way to rectify the mistake." Furthermore "you will have destroyed a source of evidence . . . often one counter-revolutionary serves as a living witness against another". And finally, "counter-revolutionaries inside Party and government organs are different from those in society at large" in that they "make enemies in general but seldom enemies in particular" because they are "somewhat removed from the masses":

"What harm is there in killing none of them? Those who are physically fit for manual labour should be reformed through labour, and those who are not should be provided for. Counter-revolutionaries are trash, they are vermin, but once in your hands, you can make them perform some kind of service for the people."

Mao added that it was not necessary to formalize this policy by law, as there might still be cases of cadres and Party members calling for the death penalty. "Ours is a policy for internal observance which need not be made public, and all we need do is carry it out as far as possible in practice." As regards the suppression of counter-revolutionaries "in society at large", Mao also said that from then on there should be fewer arrests and executions.

The existence of such a policy *vis-à-vis* members of the administration, the army or the Party does not mean that offenders belonging to such institutions are automatically exempted from punishment. Recently, for instance, five local officials from Yunnan province are reported to have been dismissed from their posts and punished "in accordance with their situation" for engaging in malpractices in order to get their relatives into university. An article on the affair in the

Yunnan Daily of 13 March 1978 commented that "those who committed offences while they themselves were enforcing the law . . . must be punished by Party disciplinary and administrative actions. As for those whose offences are serious, we must deal with them in accordance with the law."[2] Thus, when cadres commit an offence, a number of administrative sanctions may be imposed directly on them by the organization to which they belong, but in a few "serious" cases, they may be brought to court for criminal punishment.

There is no doubt, however, that this policy results in inequality of treatment between various categories of people who are charged with the same offence. Because of the importance attached to political and class background, this is even truer of punishment. Since cadres and Party members are necessarily officially regarded as having a good background, they are more likely to be treated leniently.

The process described below concerns offenders whose cases are handled by the normal law-enforcement apparatus—that is, for the most part, political offenders in "society at large".

Arrest and detention

Uniformed police officers (including the traffic police) as well as plain-clothes security officers are under the Ministry of Public Security (*gonganbu*). The Public Security apparatus is responsible for the detention and investigation of suspects and offenders.

Branches of the Public Security exist at all administrative levels (see the diagram on p. 41). In large cities, a Public Security Bureau (*gonganju*) controls police and security operations in the city. Under them are the Sub-Bureaux (*gongan fenju*) at city district level; they in turn supervise the public security stations (*gongan jieju*, also known as *paichusuo*) established at the level of "administrative streets" (or neighbourhoods—one "administrative street" corresponds to several streets). Canton city, for example, is divided into four districts which are in turn subdivided into more than 20 "administrative streets". Except for the three largest cities (Peking, Tianjin and Shanghai), which are directly under the authority of the central Government, Public Security Bureaux at city level come under the jurisdiction of the provinces' Public Security Departments (*gonganting*), which are themselves directly responsible to the (national) Ministry of Public Security.

The same structural arrangement exists in the countryside: the provinces' Public Security Departments have branches in districts and counties. At the level of the people's communes and of the production brigades (a production brigade is a subdivision of the people's commune and often corresponds to a former natural village), one or several cadres are generally responsible for public security.

In provinces and important cities, the Public Security Bureaux are split up into a number of divisions (generally more than 10), each having a particular area of responsibility.[3] One division is in charge of criminal cases; another one handles the investigation of political offenders or suspects; the "preliminary trial" division gathers pre-trial evidence and prepares trials in co-operation with court judges; another section is in charge of "reform-through-labour"—that is, of the running and control of prisons and labour camps or farms.

On 20 December 1954 the Standing Committee of the National People's Congress adopted regulations governing arrest and detention in the PRC.[4] Article 1 of the Arrest and Detention Act stipulated that, in accordance with Article 89 of the 1954 Constitution of the PRC, a citizen's freedom of person is inviolable and that "no citizen may be arrested except by the decision of a people's court or with the sanction of a people's procuratorial organ". When the Constitution was amended in 1975, the procuratorial organs were abolished and the Public Security agencies were empowered both to sanction and to make arrests—a function which they had in fact exercised since the Cultural Revolution. However, the procuratorial organs were re-established when the Constitution was revised again in March 1978 and the provisions for arrest in the 1978 Constitution read as follows: "No citizen may be arrested except by decision of a people's court or with the sanction of a people's procuratorate, and the arrest must be made by a public security organ." (Article 47)

According to the law, when a suspect is apprehended the Public Security agency handling the case must issue a "detention warrant" (*juliuzheng*), permitting the suspect to be held from 24 to 48 hours for preliminary investigation in order to establish whether there is enough evidence against him to warrant "arrest". If sufficient evidence is found, an "arrest warrant" (*daibuzheng*) is issued, permitting the unlimited detention of the person in order to establish whether there is sufficient evidence against him or her to justify prosecution.[5] In some cases the detention warrant is not necessary and an arrest warrant may be issued directly—for instance, if an offender is caught in the act of committing a crime.

However, ex-detainees and former police officials have reported that the warrants procedure has seldom been followed since the Cultural Revolution. The Public Security officers who carry out arrests at the basic (police station) level can apparently ask their senior officers for a renewal of the "detention warrant". If, after some time, they have not found enough evidence but feel that the

Table of the Law Enforcement Apparatus

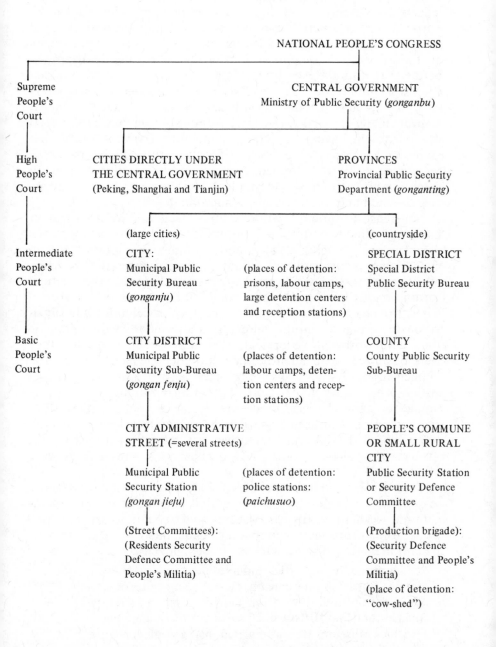

NATIONAL PEOPLE'S CONGRESS

Supreme People's Court

CENTRAL GOVERNMENT
Ministry of Public Security (*gonganbu*)

High People's Court

CITIES DIRECTLY UNDER
THE CENTRAL GOVERNMENT
(Peking, Shanghai and Tianjin)

PROVINCES
Provincial Public Security
Department (*gonganting*)

(large cities)

(countryside)

Intermediate People's Court

CITY:
Municipal Public
Security Bureau
(*gonganju*)

(places of detention:
prisons, labour camps,
large detention centers
and reception stations)

SPECIAL DISTRICT
Special District
Public Security Bureau

Basic People's Court

CITY DISTRICT
Municipal Public
Security Sub-Bureau
(*gongan fenju*)

(places of detention:
labour camps, deten-
tion centers and recep-
tion stations)

COUNTY
County Public Security
Sub-Bureau

CITY ADMINISTRATIVE
STREET (=several streets)

PEOPLE'S COMMUNE
OR SMALL RURAL
CITY

Municipal Public
Security Station
(*gongan jieju*)

(places of detention:
police stations:
(*paichusuo*)

Public Security Station
or Security Defence
Committee

(Street Committees):
(Residents Security
Defence Committee and
People's Militia)

(Production brigade):
(Security Defence
Committee and People's
Militia)
(place of detention:
"cow-shed")

case should be investigated further, they hand it over to the Public Security Sub-Bureau where preliminary detention can be further extended. At the city level, the Public Security Bureau may, reportedly, detain a suspect for a year before issuing an "arrest warrant", and this period may be extended with the approval of the province's Public Security Department. The statutory requirements of the Arrest and Detention Act also were frequently neglected before the Cultural Revolution. Jerome Cohen reports in *The Criminal Process in the People's Republic of China 1949-1963* that, according to former police officials, "police units sometimes detain criminal suspects under the SAPA (Security Administration Punishment Act) in order to circumvent the requirements of the Arrest Act" and that "most police officials are concerned only with 'breaking the case', see no need to trouble themselves about the legality of lengthy detention prior to arrest and simply detain the suspect until they are able to determine whether arrest is appropriate".[6]

Adherence to formal legal procedures seems to have been further hampered after the Cultural Revolution by the existence of "mass organizations" which have apparently assumed an important role in maintaining public order. In Canton, for instance, the "workers investigation brigades"[7] which were created during the Cultural Revolution are reported to have survived until recently as a sort of parallel police body, carrying out tasks such as detention and supervision of certain detention centers. It is also reported that although they have worked in coordination with the Public Security, they were organized independently under a unified General Command at municipal level.[8] The "workers brigades" existed in other provinces also. It is not known to what extent these organizations were officially bound to follow the legal procedures for arrest and detention. However, many cases of arbitrary arrest are said to have been made after the Cultural Revolution by either the military authorities, the "workers brigades" or other mass organizations, especially between 1967 and 1971.

Yang Rong is an example of someone arrested by a mass organization—in this instance a group of Red Guards—at the end of the Cultural Revolution. His case was reported to Amnesty International by a former prisoner who became acquainted with it while in detention himself. The account he gave is summarized here:

"Yang Rong, in his forties and a resident of Canton, was
detained in 1968 on vague charges of being 'anti-socialist'.
Until the Cultural Revolution Yang had been a secretary in
the Cultural and Historical Department of Guangdong
Province Museum. He was married, had a young daughter,

and had a good political record since he had participated in the Revolution and had the class background of office worker. He had also occasionally published poems and short articles in the *Yangcheng* evening paper.

"During the Cultural Revolution Yang joined one of the 'rebel' factions [9] of Canton and once participated in an armed fight towards the end of 1967. This experience shocked him and he decided not to involve himself in any more fighting. As this was not possible if he remained in Canton, he went to his native village for a time. Soon, however, he became worried about his work at the Museum and decided to return to Canton to see what was happening.

"At that time, members of the faction to which he had belonged were reviewing a number of internal problems. As Yang had been away without giving any reason, they suspected him of 'betrayal' and detained him after his return to Canton. Yang was locked up in a room in the Museum for questioning. The reason for his detention was suspicion of betrayal, but his accusers tried to find something from his past that could be held against him. They closely examined his articles and poems and pressed him in various ways to confess that he had 'spoken' against Chairman Mao and against socialism. He was told that his wife was also detained in the Museum and that she had already admitted this. At night, Yang could hear a woman's cries. He thought that his wife was indeed detained and had confessed under pressure. . . Although he was detained for only 10 days, as a result of his distress and of the pressure, he confessed that he had once 'spoken against socialism' [10] when he was alone with his wife, and signed a confession on which his fingerprint was marked.

"Yang was then taken by some Red Guards to Canton's Public Security Department where his confession was presented. Because of lack of evidence, the Public Security officers at first did not want to detain him. However, after several hours of discussion with the Red Guards they agreed to keep him for questioning and signed a detention warrant [*juliuzheng*] against him. His family was told to bring him clothes, blankets and articles for daily use. Yang was then sent to *Hemulang* detention center, west of Canton City, and put in a cell with two other prisoners. . . The two prisoners in his cell immediately started tormenting him with questions about his case and stole some of his belongings. Yang called

at the cell door, which only provoked more malevolence and
threats from the other two prisoners. After a few days Yang
tried to commit suicide by banging his head on the wall.
Seeing that, his two cell-mates were frightened of being
involved in any trouble and said: 'If you want to die, it is
easy, you just have to shout counter-revolutionary slogans and
you will be executed. . .'

"Yang took their words to heart and started shouting 'down
with Mao', 'down with the Party', 'long live Jiang Jieshi [Chiang
Kai-shek]', etc. Several guards arrived immediately, dragged
him out of the cell to an empty room and beat him up with
hand-cuffs to stop him shouting. He lost consciousness
and when he woke up he discovered that his feet were raised
from the floor and chained to a bar of the window. He yelled
slogans once again. The guards came back, gagged him and
also chained his hands to the window. Yang was then left
in this uncomfortable position for one day and one night
without food or water. The next day, his whole body ached
when he was unchained and he could hardly stand up. He was
given some water and the director of the detention center told
him: 'This is a dictatorship organization. You should obey
the regulations. If there is something you want to say, you
should wait for your trial.' Yang was then put into another
cell. . ."

According to this report, the detention center's authorities were
wondering after this incident whether Yang was a counter-
revolutionary or mentally deranged. When his full story became
known to the director, the latter did not consider that Yang's
original "crime" was very serious but remarked that by his
behaviour "he had now created a big problem for himself". When
Yang was questioned again after the incident, his interrogators
are reported to have said: "You wouldn't have shouted these
slogans if you hadn't already had these thoughts in your head."

Yang Rong was arrested in 1968. Amnesty International has been
told that by 1975 he had still not returned to his family.

The basic units of the Public Security structure are the "police
stations" (*paichusuo*) which exist in small country towns, villages
and in the city neighbourhoods. According to an article published in
1977 in Hong Kong,[11] in Guangdong province, when suspects are
apprehended by an officer of a "police station", they can be dealt
with in three ways:

— if they are not local residents, they are sent to a "reception station" (screening or transit detention center) from which they will be transferred to the Public Security agency where they live;

— minor offenders, such as petty thieves, may be transferred to a detention center controlled by the "Workers Inspectors Command", a civilian organization which until recently played a role in the maintenance of public order;

— if the person apprehended is suspected of a serious crime or a political offence, the case will be transferred to the level above (the Public Security Sub-Bureau) for investigation.

The arrest of political offenders takes particular forms when the country is mobilized for a political campaign. In general, such campaigns could be compared with periods of emergency when special machinery is set up to search for possible offenders. At such times, arrests at the local level are rarely motivated by the discovery of crimes: rather, they are generally carried out to comply with instructions from the central authorities on the campaign.

The 1970 "one-strike three-anti" campaign,[12] for instance, was a search for people who had committed "economic" offences, as well as for political offenders. This campaign is reported to have been launched after Mao Tsetung went to the Yan'an area during June and July 1969 and discovered that a large number of "counter-revolutionaries"—including Party members—were still "active" in words or deeds (*yanxing*). Following a decision by the CCP Central Committee, documents outlining the aims of the campaign were sent to the provinces in the summer and autumn of 1969. One of the documents gave instructions to "strike at active counter-revolutionaries" (*daji xianxing fangeming*), either "hidden" or "active" in words or deeds. Another document was aimed at eliminating corruption (*fan tanwu*), waste (*fan langfei*) and speculation (*fan touji daoba*). These two sets of objectives were summed up in one slogan, "one-strike three-antis" (*yida sanfan*), which gave its name to the movement. In the course of the campaign, many people were detained for investigation without normal legal procedures being used.

Investigation

There are generally three main phases in the full investigation of a case which will eventually be brought to trial. The first is the preliminary search for criminal evidence by the body making the arrest. Evidence may consist of material evidence, witnesses' testimonies, and/or the accused's confession. The second stage is the examination of evidence at a higher level, including interrogation of the witnesses and of the accused. The third phase is the interrogation of the offender by the authorities in charge of preparing the trial.

In the case of political defendants, the whole investigation relies mainly on the intensive interrogation of both the accused and people possibly connected with the case. It is common in such cases for criminal evidence to be largely based on numerous autobiographies or reports on past behaviour, friendships, relationships and activities that the accused must write while in detention. What is written is checked step by step with possible witnesses or against the reports of people who may be investigated in connection with the case. At this stage, however, other factors—such as a change of policy or the discovery of decisive evidence—may prompt either release or conviction. Throughout this process, it is of the greatest importance that offenders "confess"—that is, recognize that what they have done or said is a "crime" for which they must be "reformed".

Detention may therefore last as long as is necessary to gather sufficient evidence to make the accused thoroughly confess his or her "crime" before the case is brought to court. This applies also to ordinary criminal cases. A Japanese journalist, Tadashi Ito, reported in 1977 that some Japanese lawyers who visited China in 1975 and attended the court proceedings of a man charged with embezzlement learned that three years had passed between his arrest and his prosecution. The reason for this delay, Mr Ito said, "is that Public Security officers and the judges carry out thorough investigations of the crime, including holding discussions with the people to learn their views, and move to prosecute only after a decision has been reached".[13]

According to the 1954 Arrest and Detention Act, a suspect may not be detained before a "detention warrant" or an "arrest warrant" has been issued. The Act also stipulates that, in order to search for criminal evidence, the arresting organizations may, while arresting and detaining a suspect, search his or her person, belongings, home, and those of other people or other related places (Article 9).

A young man named Zhang,[14] arrested in May 1970 in connection with his participation in a political study group (or "clique", *jituan*), was detained as a result of the accidental interception of a letter sent to him by a friend. The letter was handed over to the Public Security authorities of the county where Zhang was living. The county passed it down to the relevant people's commune which, in turn, gave it to the Public Security personnel of the production brigade where Zhang had been assigned to work.

On receipt of the letter—in which Zhang's friend referred to their studies of Marxist books and to the need to remain "quiet" now that the situation was very tense—the brigade's security personnel decided on the following course of action: they organized a"study class of Mao Tsetung Thought"[15] in the brigade's school for all the young people in the brigade, including Zhang. At the end of the study session everyone was sent away, except Zhang and two other young men. One of the two was a friend of Zhang's and the other an active "educated youth". The three were locked up separately in different classrooms for interrogation. Zhang was interrogated by members of the brigade's Security Defence group (*baoweizu*) and militia. They questioned him about his relationship with people outside the brigade. It did not occur to Zhang that the questioning was connected with the Marxist-Leninist study group that he and his friends had organized, as during the previous years it had been common for young people to organize such groups and discuss politics.

In the course of the interrogation a member of the militia discreetly placed a piece of paper under his cigarette pack for Zhang. The paper advised Zhang to confess immediately about the "spy ring" which he and his friends had formed. The militiaman's gesture may have been well-intentioned as, according to official policy, "confession deserves leniency, resistance deserves severity."

Questioning continued for a week in the brigade headquarters, but Zhang did not admit to any "crime". After a week, the head of the brigade's Security Defence group told him that he was not being "frank" and that, after investigation by the brigade and the commune, and with the approval of the County Public Security authorities, a decision had been taken to transfer him to a "reception station"[16] "so that he confess [*jiaodai*]".

At the reception station, his case was taken over by the County Public Security authorities. The county's interrogators started asking him new kinds of question. They were no longer about "spying" but about whether Zhang and his friends had said anything critical of Mao or of official policy. Zhang explained that the group's purpose had been to make a general evaluation of the Cultural Revolution. Several times he was asked to give written accounts of their discussions, and he always wrote the same thing. After a week, since Zhang had not yet admitted committing any offence, it was decided to transfer him again so that he could "reflect on his crimes".

A "detention warrant" was then issued, which Zhang was given to sign when he was transferred to the county detention center. In the center, he was first held for one month in solitary confinement. Since his arrest, his family had known nothing of his fate and he was not allowed to write to them until a month later when he was put in a communal cell. During his month in isolation, Zhang was interrogated every day from 8.30 a.m. to 12 noon and from the beginning of the afternoon till 6.30 p.m. In the evenings he had to write detailed accounts of his past activities. He soon realized that the investigation was also being conducted outside the detention center, as Public Security officials from other counties came to interrogate him. Their questions were more specific and he guessed that his friends were also being investigated. (He learned later that about 10 of them had also been arrested in other counties.) The authorities were comparing evidence obtained from what each of them said or wrote. Zhang alleges that a "political instructor" (*guanjiaoyuan*) from the detention center told him that he was "late in confessing", that he was a "counter-revolutionary according to the sixth clause of the Public Security" regulations and told him about people who had been executed under that clause.

Zhang had not so far admitted to anything which could be considered a "crime". However, he was apparently frightened by these threats, made an unsuccessful attempt to escape and also tried to commit suicide (he tied pieces of his bed-sheet together to form a rope). This was discovered and he was then placed in a large cell with about 30 other detainees. Before his transfer to the communal cell, he was admonished by the authorities and told that the detention center was a former Guomindang prison and conditions had been terrible under the previous régime and that the present government, on the other hand, was lenient: instead of punishing him they were going to transfer him to a large cell and let him "study". Investigation continued for four months after his transfer to the communal cell. At first Zhang was still questioned morning and afternoon, but interrogation gradually decreased to about one hour a day during the next four months. Zhang was told to address his interrogator as "judge" (*faguan*). At each session what he said was written down and he had to put his thumbprint on the written records of interrogation. After four months, a final interrogation session took place. The "judge" asked Zhang whether he admitted that his "words" were "anti-Central Committee, anti-Mao and anti-Lin Biao". Zhang only admitted that his "thinking was reactionary"; he had to put his thumbprint on the record of what he had said. This was the last time he was interrogated. For the next eighteen months he spent most of his time in daily "study, criticism and self-criticism sessions", held in the cell with other prisoners, to make them "reflect on their crimes", "raise their consciousness" and confess. No "arrest warrant" or indictment was ever issued against Zhang and he was finally released after two years without being given a proper explanation.

Zhang's case is typical of many other cases of detention at that time. He was arrested merely for his participation in a Marxist-Leninist study group and held two years "for investigation" without being formally charged with any particular offence. After his arrest, the authorities did not notify his family of his detention. He himself was able to do so when he was allowed to write, more than a month and a half after his arrest, but he has subsequently reported that his family never received his first letter. Article 5 of the Arrest and Detention Act specifies that, after arrest, the organization carrying out arrest shall notify the family of the person arrested of the reason for arrest and the place of detention, "unless such notification will hinder investigation or there is no way of notifying the family". In Zhang's case, there was apparently nothing to prevent the authorities from notifying his family, except for the fact that legal procedures were generally ignored after the Cultural Revolution.

Zhang's case indicates some of the methods used during investigation. Usually the accused are not told precisely what is held against them and are not informed of the developments of the investigation. Their correspondence, if allowed, is censored, and visits are generally not permitted until prosecution starts. The Law on Reform Through Labour[17] also provides that, for the sake of the investigation, detainees "whose cases are major" must be held in isolation (solitary confinement) and that those involved in the same or related cases must be held separately from one another. ex pnt fato onu

In the case of political offenders, the interrogation of the accused plays a particularly important role. In between two sessions of interrogation, the accused is asked to write reports on past activities which may provide useful details for the interrogators, and which will be followed up by more questions and more requests for written reports. The accused cannot refuse to write such reports because this is officially considered a "lack of cooperation with the government" and is practically treated as an offence in itself. The use of coercion to extract "forced" confessions is officially prohibited, but not the practice of obliging detainees to write autobiographies and reports about their past activities. As pre-trial detention is unlimited, the accused is easily led to include self-incriminating evidence in reports before being brought to trial.[18]

In the course of investigation, the search for or examination of *prima facie* evidence is generally made at several levels. In the countryside, for instance, if a suspect is discovered in a production brigade, the brigade members responsible for security will inform the people's commune security committee. The commune's committee makes a preliminary investigation and if suspicions are confirmed writes a report to the County Public Security Bureau. The County Bureau may then issue a "detention warrant" to detain the suspect and start an investigation to find out whether there are enough grounds for "arrest". However, if the case is important, the County Bureau will refer the decision to "arrest" to a higher level: the District Public Security Bureau. The District Bureau in turn makes its own investigation before taking a decision, and sends investigators to the suspect's brigade, interrogates the suspect, witnesses, people possibly connected with the case, and so on. This process usually takes a long time. The system of checking at various levels is apparently aimed at preventing miscarriages of justice, but it obviously involves arbitrary detention.

Although, according to the legal procedures, the suspect may not be detained without at least a "detention warrant", it is not unusual during political campaigns for the suspect to be detained for interrogation from the time of discovery in the brigade, and for the brigade's officials themselves to make a preliminary investigation, finding witnesses and recording their statements. Such practices have led to arbitrary arrests in the past.

During political campaigns, the pressure to find "class enemies" is particularly intense and arbitrary detention occurs frequently. The process of investigation takes particular forms at such periods. "Special groups" (*zhuananzu*) are formed at local level to strengthen the Public Security agencies during the time of the campaign. In addition, "work teams" (*gongzuodui*)—also specially created for the campaign—may be sent to particular areas. They are composed of experienced cadres and Party members, and have the task of explaining official policy to local cadres and helping them to mobilize the population for the campaign. These teams are sent all over the country. They may be dispatched to selected areas where particular problems have been reported or where local cadres do not show sufficient initiative in "carrying out the class struggle".

The process of investigation during a campaign generally develops along the following lines.[19] With or without the help of the work teams, the local cadres first study the specific instructions of the campaign and other related documents, examine the records of people living in the area and make a preliminary assessment of who might be investigated according to the instructions of the campaign. At the same time, posters are displayed publicly, explaining the aims of the campaign in the form of slogans and urging the "masses" to "expose" (denounce) "bad elements" and "counter-revolutionaries". A series of mobilization meetings is organized, during which the masses are encouraged to denounce all unusual behaviour and activities. Known wrongdoers may be criticized for their past misdeeds during the meetings. Such mobilization generally provides the cadres with new denunciations, which can be made publicly during the meetings, or privately. This process, which may be repeated several times in the course of the campaign, is described in official Chinese terminology as the "four greats" or the four methods of carrying out "struggle by reasoning": "great debate" (*da ming*), "great blooming" (*da fang*), "big character posters" (*dazibao*) and "great denunciation" (*dajiefa*).

Some suspects may be detained from the beginning of the campaign and, on the basis of information provided by denunciation, other people may be detained for investigation in the course of it. Various investigation methods may be used. The milder methods are those involving "persuasion-education" (*shuofu jiaoyu*). This can, for instance, consist of obligatory attendance at a "study class of Mao Tsetung Thought",[20] or "isolation in order to make a self-examination". This would generally apply to minor offenders who have a good background and can be persuaded rapidly to recognize their mistakes.

Those who resist and those who are suspected of more serious offences will generally be put immediately in detention. In the countryside, the most rudimentary places of detention are the cowsheds (*niulan*) which are frequently used during campaigns. During interrogation, the suspect is repeatedly exhorted to "expose" in detail past behaviour and activities as well as those of other people.

Meanwhile, large or small meetings are organized in the brigade (village) for people connected with one particular suspect. They are asked to expose and, sometimes, to write a report on the suspect after the meetings. From this combination of statements and from the interrogation of the suspects the authorities may find evidence against the latter. If evidence is found, larger meetings are organized to announce what is known about the offenders and to invite further criticism from the masses. The purpose of such meetings is to "raise the consciousness of the masses" and to try to obtain more evidence about the people detained.

Although official instructions are often given not to extract confessions under compulsion,[21] it seems that the means used to obtain statements and confessions often overstep these bounds.[22] Intimidation is the most common form of compulsion. The tension created by some campaigns is such that denunciations and false statements may be made by people who are afraid that they themselves will be detained. In some cases, it is reported that non-stop interrogation (*chelunzhan*) is used to "crack" a case. In addition, "struggle meetings" may be organized specifically to make the accused admit their crimes. Such meetings can last a very long time and may become so tense that insults, threats, various humiliations and even blows are used by people in the audience to put pressure on the offender to confess in the presence of the cadres.

The practice of sending "work teams" to the villages towards the end of a campaign is an indication that arbitrariness can occur in the course of it. These teams differ from those sent at the beginning of a campaign. Like their forerunners, they are composed of cadres and Party members, but their task is to help local cadres to "apply the policy" *(luoshi zhengce)*—an implicit recognition that the "policy" may not have been applied properly during the campaign. They help to determine who among those detained should be held for prosecution, who should be released and who should be given light punishment on the spot. According to a popular saying, these teams are called "the lucky doctors who come to treat at the end of the illness".

In the words of one former cadre, the obsession to do "a good job" in implementing a campaign is shown at each level by increased pressure on the lower level to find offenders. At the bottom, such pressure is put on the masses that many may denounce other people in order to save everybody from the "disease" of the campaign.

These campaigns are not, however, carried out with the same intensity in all villages and areas. In some places no arrests may be made, especially if no work teams have been sent to the area. In other places the campaign may die down for a variety of reasons, including the possible reluctance of local cadres to organize such mobilization.

Trials

China has four categories of courts at different administrative levels—basic people's courts, intermediate people's courts, high people's courts and, at national level, the Supreme People's Court. The local courts deal with criminal and civil cases. The Supreme Court deals mainly with cases of national importance and death penalty cases. When a local court passes a death sentence, the case is supposed to be brought before the Supreme Court for approval before sentence can be carried out. China seems, in addition, to have kept special courts, such as military courts, courts in mining areas and railway courts, [23] which existed before the Cultural Revolution.

The revised text of the Constitution adopted in March 1978 does not restore the guarantee of judicial independence laid down in Article 78 of the 1954 Constitution, which had been removed from the Constitution when it was first amended in 1975. Part of that

Article read: "the people's courts are independent, subject only to law". Article 41 of the 1978 Constitution simply states that the courts "exercise judicial authority".

Chinese judges and officials have stressed on many occasions since the 1950s that the courts' work is supervised by the Chinese Communist Party (CCP). In 1958, the Deputy Chairman of the China Political and Legal Affairs Society, Wu Te-feng, replied to criticisms[24] of the Party's interference in the work of the courts by saying:

". . . In China, the legal system has been created under the leadership of the Communist Party, in accordance with the principles of Marxism-Leninism and the experience of the people themselves in the course of class struggle . . .

". . . We all know that laws have to be administered according to the policies of the State, and it is the Communist Party which is the most capable of deciding such policies in the interests of all the People. The Party does not interfere with the courts' independent trials as long as they adhere to the policies of the State. Is there anything wrong with such leadership and supervision? "[25]

These principles were reaffirmed more recently by Chinese legal officials. In May 1974, the Chairman of the Guangdong Institute of Law and Political Science stated in an interview that "the principles on which the court's work is based are Party policy and the law of the State".[26] Two American lawyers were told in October 1974 by members of the Law Faculty of Peking University that the principle of the trial system is "to serve the dictatorship of the proletariat. It should serve the people and attack the people's enemy."[27] In August 1977, during a conference attended by regional legal cadres and Party leaders of Heilongjiang province, the provincial Party Secretary called on all Party Committees of the province to strengthen their leadership over judicial work.[28] According to a radio broadcast from Nanjing on 11 November 1977, the Nanjing Municipal Party Committee decided on a number of "exemplary cases" deserving "lenient or severe treatment".[29]

Thus, Party leadership in judicial work is an established practice. The Party Committees at certain administrative levels exercise this supervisory function through their departments of legal and political affairs. In political cases, investigators and Party officials cooperate closely until prosecution begins. The judges seldom reject the recommendations of these combined authorities, generally because they share the same viewpoint but also because they are responsible to political authorities. In any case, they cannot resist on the grounds of procedure because the dossiers prepared by the Public Security would normally include "sufficient evidence". The court judgment, although passed by the courts, is itself the subject of consultation between the judges, the investigators and Party officials involved in the case.

The Austrian Minister of Justice, Christian Broda, who visited China with an Austrian delegation in January 1977, reported the explanation of criminal procedure given by a judge from Shanghai High Court, Liu Tong-lu:

"A case is first investigated by the Security authorities and then forwarded to a court which will pronounce the judgment. The trial will be conducted in the presence of the defendant, and he must be heard. He is also given the indictment . . .

"When a criminal offence has been committed, the investigation has to determine whether the accused has committed the act, so that a proposal can be worked out. The responsible official writes a report to the management group. If the offence is a serious one, the court dealing with it will report to the next higher court. Sentence may never be passed by a judge—only by a collective. The masses will then be informed of the sentence. This means that the treatment of a case serves to educate the masses. The convicted person is then handed over to the Security authorities and re-educated through labour."[30]

The following factors are taken into account when the court judgment is decided upon.

One of the main principles of the "Party's policy" in judicial work is that "leniency is given to those who confess their crimes and severe punishment is given to those who refuse to do so".[31] When a case is assigned to a judge, the dossier generally already includes a written confession made by the defendant. As has been said, the main purpose of unlimited pre-trial detention is to make the accused report in detail on their past activities and write confessions. The constant pressure to confess may even result in confessions of non-existent offences. A High Court judge from Shanghai confirmed this during an interview in November 1976: "Even though a defendant has admitted his guilt and confessed his crime, the judges feel they have to go further. They understand that sometimes people confess when they have not committed the crime. It may be because of the pressure of the group."[32] The judge, however, admitted: "There is rarely a prosecution where there is not a confession or a guilty plea."[33]

Since the Cultural Revolution, a process of "consultation with the masses" has been introduced into judicial practice. Article 41 of the 1978 Constitution states: ". . . With regard to major counter-revolutionary or criminal cases, the masses should be drawn in for discussion and suggestions."

This process of consultation consists of organizing discussions with the accused's colleagues at work or neighbours before he or she is brought to trial, or, sometimes, of organizing a public trial after judgment has been passed (see below). Such consultations, however, have no decisive influence on the judgment, but rather are an educative exercise for the "masses". In the words of legal officials from Peking, the fact that the masses are asked to give their opinions "does not mean that we would listen and follow what they say. The judges have to make an analysis of the opinion of the masses and the final decision is made by the People's Courts."[34] Usually the accused is not present during a "mass discussion" on the case.[35]

Another important factor in the decision is the determination of whether the defendant belongs to the "people" or is an "enemy of the people". For this, class status is taken into account and past history examined in detail. Class origin is particularly important for political offenders since a "bad" family background makes them automatically potential "enemies of the people".

Finally, the "seriousness" of the "crime" itself will be weighed according to two sets of criteria: first, the official policy at the time (which has defined as "criminal" certain attitudes or acts) and the local situation (whether these attitudes or acts are a particularly serious problem in the area—in which case they must be dealt with severely): second, everything to do with the defendant's background and attitude (class status, past history, willingness to confess and repent) and with the opinions of the masses. On this basis, the sentence will be decided shortly before trial.

Trials are a mere formality: rather than "trials", they are, in fact, meetings to announce the sentence. A judge from Shanghai, describing a case of embezzlement, stated in 1976: "The day after the judgment was decided upon, the trial took place. It was an open trial in the factory. The defendant confessed his crime. Friends of the defendant spoke. The trial lasted two hours."[36]

The 1978 Constitution stipulates that "all cases in the people's courts are heard in public except those involving special circumstances, as prescribed by law" (Article 41). This was also laid down in the 1954 Constitution but had been removed from the 1975 Constitution. Cases in which there was to be no public trial were specified in 1956: they were those "relating to state secrets" or to the "intimate life of the parties" or cases involving juvenile offenders.[37] Evidently the provision according to which cases "relating to state secrets" should not be tried publicly has been interpreted broadly. In all cases of convicted political offenders known to Amnesty International, the defendants were either tried *in camera* or given "mass public trials" where no defence was possible. In other political cases, no official information has been disclosed for years about the offenders' fate and often nothing is known about their trial.[38] Trials can be divided into three main categories:

1 Closed trials: It is reported that the majority of political offenders have closed trials. Generally the defendant is taken to the court, but may also be called to a room in the place of detention. One or several judges and investigators may be present. The judge gives a summary of the case and asks the accused whether he agrees or has anything to add. Sometimes the accused is asked to say, of his own accord, what punishment the crime deserves and will generally express the hope that the Government in its "leniency" will allow the opportunity for self-reform despite the "serious crime". Then the sentence is announced and the defendant signs the judgment. After judgment, the sentence will sometimes be announced publicly through an official court notice posted in a public place.

2 Open trials (*kaiting*): During these the defendant can summon relatives, friends or neighbours to speak in his or her defence. To the extent that this procedure is used, however, it applies mainly in criminal cases and cases of minor importance and has been rarely resorted to in the decade from 1966 to 1976. These "trials" in any case take place after the sentence has been decided, in the form of small-scale public meetings held in the defendant's work unit.

3 "Mass public trials":[39] These trials take two forms: *xuanpan dahui* "big meeting to announce the sentence", and *gongsheng* "mass trial". Both involve a very large number of participants—up to tens of thousands of people—and are organized to mobilize the population and educate it through negative examples. The *xuanpan dahui* is generally used for a group (sometimes large) of offenders belonging to various categories who are tried simultaneously. The *gongsheng*, on the other hand, involves fewer offenders; the purpose behind it, too, is to criticize harshly and "struggle against" the defendants. The *gongsheng* are staged especially for political offenders who have not yet thoroughly admitted their crimes or showed repentance whom the authorities want to use as an example. The *gongsheng* is a severe ordeal for the accused. It can last for a very long time and violence may be used against the accused. The *gongsheng* occur mainly during political campaigns but may be held at other times also for cases involving the death penalty or long-term imprisonment.

The accused's right to defence, which was removed from the

Constitution when it was amended in 1975, was re-established in the 1978 Constitution. However, the function of defence lawyers, which existed in the mid-1950s in the PRC, has now disappeared. According to a Chinese judge, this is because the people know the published laws and regulations and the accused "has the full right to speak for himself" or to ask other people "to speak in his defence".[40] The right to defence is, in practice, very limited. As has already been said, political defendants are not usually tried publicly. Furthermore, they know that if they defend themselves against the accusations—except perhaps to plead mitigating circumstances—they will only make their case worse, so they generally refrain from doing so. Often, their neighbours or colleagues would rather criticize than defend them for fear of being criticized themselves. Only if the accused confess and repent would relatives and others dare to stress extenuating circumstances.

Thus, if those accused of political offences defend themselves against the accusations, this can be treated as an aggravating circumstance. Examples of this are occasionally given in the official accounts of court judgments which are periodically posted publicly in Chinese cities. One public notice from Guangdong province High People's Court, dated 18 February 1978, announced that a political offender named He Chunshu had been sentenced to death for writing and distributing a "counter-revolutionary" leaflet. The notice specified that He Chunshu had "obstinately refused to admit his crime", that the "wrath of the people was very great" and that the court therefore sentenced him to immediate execution.[41]

Penalties

There are various kinds of informal penalties in China for political offenders. The mildest and most common, based on "persuasive" methods, are used for people who have simply committed "minor mistakes" or whom the authorities want to warn before subjecting them to more serious punishment. The main informal sanctions are:[42]

— Criticism: this can be made privately by several cadres or publicly in the presence of a fairly large number of the offender's neighbours or colleagues, and the offender has to make an oral or written self-criticism, or both.

— "Struggle" meetings: the aim of a "struggle" is to denounce the accused publicly and intimidate him or her in front of a large audience, using more violence than during "criticism" meetings. A "struggle" often involves threats, humiliations and even beatings.[43]

For more serious offences, China has both "administrative" and "criminal" penalties. The first category applies to offenders who are not officially regarded as "criminals". These "administrative" penalties can be inflicted by simple police order or by decision of a work/neighbourhood/Party unit, without a court decision. The "criminal" penalties apply to offences officially defined as "crimes" and are imposed by the courts on police recommendation. In practice however, there is little qualitative difference between "administrative" penalties and many "criminal" penalties. The main punishments affecting political offenders are the following:

a Administrative penalties (*xingzheng chufen*)

— "Supervised labour" or work "under supervision of the masses" (*pei junzhong kanguan*), which means that offenders may remain in society but are under surveillance: they have to engage in productive work, attend political sessions and report regularly to the cadres. For Party members, this would be "work under supervision of the Party" (*liudang chakan*). For them and for members of the administration, teaching and medical personnel, demotion in rank or position can be a supplementary penalty.

— "Rehabilitation through labour" (*laodong jiaoyang*), for which the offenders are sent to special camps (or farms) to labour and "re-educate" themselves. This is quite similar to "reform through labour" (see below), although it often involves slightly better detention conditions and is regarded as a milder punishment because it carries less stigma.

b Criminal penalties (*xingshi chufen*)

— "Control", which is, in practice, similar to "supervised labour" since the offender remains in society, but which is imposed by a court on people convicted of an offence. It is often applied to offenders who have previously been given an informal or administrative punishment and whose behaviour has not improved.

— A term of imprisonment, generally carried out in a "reform through labour" (*laodong gaizao)* institution (camp, prison or farm).

— Life imprisonment, generally served in a prison.

— Death penalty suspended for two years, during which time the offender's attitude is observed to see whether commutation may be warranted. The sentence is generally carried out in a prison.

— Death penalty followed by immediate execution.

The decision as to which of these punishments to inflict is determined by the general characteristics of a case rather than by the nature of the specific offence. For instance, punishing the same offence by either "rehabilitation through labour" or "reform through labour" (which are rather similar) may depend on the nature of the "contradiction" reflected by the case—that is, whether the offender is classified as belonging to the "people" or to the "enemy". The same offence may be treated in the first case as a "mistake", in the second as a "crime". However, there are no strict legal standards to help in making that distinction and judges, police and Party officials have wide discretion as regards judgment, especially in political cases.

Appeal and review

Chinese law allows the defendant to make one appeal against conviction to a court higher than the one that passed the sentence. [44] Political defendants seldom appeal. Just as a refusal to confess is considered an aggravating factor when sentence is decided upon, so may an appeal be similarly regarded and result in an increased sentence.

As well as the appeal permitted by law, a process of review can be undertaken while the offender is serving sentence. It may be undertaken by the offender, or by relatives with the offender's permission, or by the authorities themselves. Political prisoners, however, seek redress through this procedure even more rarely than through appeal. Usually, they venture to ask for review only if strong evidence that the charges were unfounded has been discovered or in special circumstances, such as those described below.

Since 1949, several national reviews of cases have been initiated by the central authorities. One is reported to have begun in 1956 when the first formal evaluation since 1949 of the "suppression of counter-revolutionaries" was made. In his report presented in June 1956 to the National People's Congress,[45] the Minister of Public Security, Luo Ruiqing, admitted that some "mistakes had been made in the suppression of counter-revolutionaries". Efforts were consequently made to trace cases of prisoners unfairly sentenced. Although no statistics are available on the general result of this review, it seems that in many cases very mild penalties were substituted for the original sentence of imprisonment.[46] The case that follows, however, is an example of an unsuccessful attempt made by a prisoner at that period.

According to a former prisoner, a man named Ding Songshan was arrested in 1952 in Zhongqing (Sichuan province) on a charge of being an "international spy" and sentenced to 10 years of "reform through labour". Ding had been a member of the Nationalist (Guomindang) administration in Zhongqing during the civil war. After the Communist forces entered Zhongqing, the new authorities told Ding to stay at his post, which he did without trouble until 1952. At that point, he took a month's leave to visit his native place, Wuhan (Hubei province), but returned to Zhongqing four days after the end of his leave. This led to his arrest and the accusation that he was a spy. In 1956, Ding was in a labour-camp in north-eastern China. The news that cases would be reviewed was announced in the camp. Meetings were organized and the prisoners who had grievances about their cases were invited to speak up. Ding consequently wrote a report on his case which was transmitted to the local county court. The court is reported to have replied, without elaborating, that what Ding had written was "different from the facts". The reply concluded by saying that if his "performance" were good he could be granted an early release; if his "performance" were not good he would be released at the expiration of his term. As Ding was apparently old and not strong physically, his work "performance" was not very good. Consequently, he was released only in 1962, when his term expired.

It would seem that the court's conclusion gave grounds for Ding's claim that he was innocent, because a "real" spy would not be promised early release if there were strong evidence against him. Moreover, one can assume that the camp authorities would not have allowed him to lodge a complaint if he had no good reason for doing so. In any event, the way in which the review was handled is significant. The court did not rule on the basis of criminal procedure and did not commit itself in substance, but in practice delegated the decision to the camp authorities. Moreover, the court gave no explanation of its reasons for rejecting Ding's case, apart from the remark that his report "differed from the facts". Ding therefore had no possibility of defending his case further.

In 1959, a similar process of review, affecting the "rightists", [47] was decided on by the CCP Central Committee and the Government on the occasion of the tenth anniversary of the establishment of the People's Republic of China.[48] As in the case of Ding, however, the "reversal of their cases" was made conditional on their good behaviour in "work and study"[49] while they were undergoing their punishment.

Another large-scale review of cases took place after Lin Biao's purge in 1971. It seems, however, to have been far more effective in prompting the release of political detainees who were not yet tried or sentenced than in releasing convicted prisoners. The review of prisoners' cases was sometimes very slow[50] and was not carried out thoroughly.[51]

After the purge of the "gang of four" in October 1976, efforts were made to correct transgressions which they or their "followers" were alleged to have committed. Many examples of "reversal of the wrong verdicts" passed while the "gang of four" was in power were given by official sources in 1977 and early 1978.[52] Most of the cases publicized concerned intellectuals, workers or cadres. Among them was that of a preliminary trial examiner from Peking Municipal Public Security Bureau who claimed to have been arrested in November 1967 on charges of trying "to shield a criminal" and to have been submitted to "fascist-type interrogations" in order to force a confession. He further stated that his "persecution" continued after he was released from prison, but did not give the date of his release.[53] The total number of those rehabilitated since the fall of the "gang of four" has not been disclosed, but partial figures have been given. On 13 March 1978, for instance, the official press reported that since 1976 more than 10,000 "victims of the gang of four" had been rehabilitated in Shanghai, some posthumously.[54]

These special reviews (which are due to changes of policy) and judicial reviews are not the only means by which prisoners' sentences can be altered: these can be changed at any time by the authorities while they are being served. However, such "reviews" are not related to guilt or innocence, but to prisoners' behaviour during imprisonment. They are, in addition, used to impose either reduced or heavier sentences.[55]

The death penalty

Most of the offences listed in the Act of the PRC for Punishment of Counter-Revolution (1951)[56] may be punished by the death penalty, in some cases with the stipulation "when the circumstances of the cases are major". They include, for instance, treason, insurrection, espionage and major "counter-revolutionary" acts. However, Article 14 of the Act provides that those offenders who have "atoned" for their crimes, or who were originally coerced into committing them, or who voluntarily surrendered to the authorities may be exempted from punishment or given a reduced punishment.

In addition to "major counter-revolutionary crimes", the other offences listed in published laws as liable to the death penalty are offences of corruption when the amount involved is 100,000,000 *yuan* or more,[57] buying state economic intelligence for private gain or obtaining the same by force,[58] and very serious cases of counterfeiting state bank-notes "for counter-revolutionary purposes" or for private gain.[59]

Despite the lack of references in the published laws to other common-law offences, official documents and statements by Chinese judges reveal that the death penalty may also be imposed for other crimes, such as murder and sexual offences.

During an interview with two American lawyers in October 1974, members of the Law Faculty of Peking University stated:

"Capital punishment is very rarely used. It is applied only to very serious cases, such as counter-revolutionary cases, assassination, and serious cases of murder, depending upon the intent and the result . . . It is subject to the approval of the Central Government . . . It is not a good way to carry out our proletariat dictatorship by killing people."[60]

Only in the cases of minors and pregnant women is the death penalty apparently not applicable. The "Lectures on the General Principles of Criminal Law of the People's Republic of China", published in 1957 by the Central Political-Legal Cadres' School in Peking, referred to a text approved by the Ministry of Justice which read in part as follows:

"For the protection of the life and normal development of a child in the womb a criminal who is pregnant generally shall not be sentenced to death. If death alone can pacify the people's anger, it [the death penalty] shall be pronounced one year after the birth of the child. . ."[61]

As previously stated, Chinese law provides for one appeal to a superior court. In capital cases, there is normally an automatic review by a higher court than the one which passed sentence, even if the defendant does not appeal. Moreover, in July 1957 the Standing Committee of the National People's Congress adopted a resolution requiring all death sentences passed by local courts to be approved by the Supreme People's Court before execution could be carried out.[62]

It seems, however, that the procedure requiring approval by the Supreme Court has generally not been followed between 1966 and 1976. It is reported that, after the Cultural Revolution, the power to order execution devolved upon the basic people's court (courts at county and city district level). During an interview in August 1975 with Reuter's correspondent, Peter Griffiths, the Deputy-Director of Tianjin High People's Court, named Hao, mentioned a case of execution in which the death sentence had apparently been passed by a basic court and ratified by an intermediate court. He apparently did not say that the sentence had been further approved by the Supreme Court. The case was that of a double murderer. Hao explained that the man was permitted to appeal to an intermediate court, but his sentence was ratified and, after a mass rally to "criticize and repudiate" him, he was shot by a policeman on one of the city's several execution sites. Hao said that the murderer had "vicious motivation" and had aroused "great indignation among the masses". According to him, only a "small handful" of criminals faced execution; rapists and murderers were liable to be shot, but the punishment depended far more on the circumstances of the case and the character of the accused.[63]

The information available on recent capital cases generally gives little indication as to whether the National People's Congress 1957 Resolution requiring approval of death sentences by the Supreme Court is still applied. However, in 1977, a judge from Shanghai High Court, interviewed by the editor of the Swedish newspaper *Dagens Nyheter* stated that Supreme Court authorization was necessary for the carrying out of each death sentence.[64]

Since quite early in the history of the PRC it has been the practice in some cases for the death sentence to be suspended for a period of two years. This suspended sentence seems to be used as a different punishment from the death sentence followed by immediate execution. During the two years' suspension, offenders undergo a program of reform and their behaviour during this period will determine the final decision as to whether or not execution will take place. If the offender "repents" and "shows willingness to reform", the death sentence may be commuted.

The criteria determining whether an offender sentenced to death should be executed or benefit from a stay of execution are loosely defined. Chinese legal officials often say that the "seriousness" of a crime and whether it provokes the "great indignation of the masses" are decisive as regards the carrying out of the death sentence.

Professor Han Yu-tung, the Deputy Director of the Law Institute of the Chinese Academy of Social Sciences, was more precise about the matter: in February 1978 he stated: ". . . it is not yet possible to abolish capital punishment in China. But, our policy also stipulates that . . . in cases where it is marginal whether to execute, under no circumstances should there be an execution."[65] He quoted Chairman Mao about the factors determining whether execution is necessary or not:

"Those who owe blood debts or are guilty of other
extremely serious crimes and have to be executed to assuage
the people's anger and those who have caused extremely
serious harm to the national interest must be unhesitatingly
sentenced to death and executed without delay.

"As for those whose crimes deserve capital punishment
but who owe no blood debts and are not bitterly hated

by the people or who have done serious but not extremely serious harm to the national interest, the policy to follow is to hand down the death sentence, grant a two-year reprieve and subject them to forced labour to see how they behave."

Between 1966 and 1976, it seems that offenders' cases were handled according to normal legal procedures mainly when there was political stability in the country, and that harsh measures—including "exemplary" public executions—were used at moments of political tension. Reports referring to periods of internal struggle and disorder, such as the Cultural Revolution, give some information on executions carried out immediately after mass public trials.[66] It has also been reported that a large number of executions were carried out during some of the political campaigns which marked the end of the Cultural Revolution.

During the "one-strike three-anti" campaign,[67] for instance, a group of about 40 people in Canton were said to have been executed immediately after a mass public trial in the spring of 1970. More than 60 people were tried, including several accused of having committed murder during the Cultural Revolution. A summary of the verdicts appeared later in official notices posted in the streets of the city. Numerous executions are reported to have been carried out throughout the country during that campaign.

It is also alleged that public executions are carried out in China's most important cities before the annual festivals: National Day (1 October), Labour Day (1 May), the Chinese New Year and Spring festival; they are seen as a deterrent to possible disorders on these occasions.

Public executions apparently generally take place immediately after the sentence has been pronounced during a mass meeting which may be attended by several hundreds or thousands of people. In such cases, the accused's hands are tied behind the back and, depending on local practice, the feet or other parts of the body may also be bound. A placard is usually fixed on the back, on which the prisoner's name, crime and sometimes the word "death" circled in red are inscribed. The accused kneels down, back turned to the executioner. The execution is then carried out by shooting by one or more Public Security officers or by soldiers.

In the case of executions which are not carried out in public, it seems that the length of time between sentencing and execution varies, depending on the decision of the local authorities. However, sometimes, apparently, execution has taken place immediately after sentencing.[68]

Official accounts of executions in China are rare and statistics about death sentences are not available. However, travellers to China occasionally report seeing official public notices announcing executions or death sentences. Since the purge of the "gang of four" in October 1976, the international press has reported the appearance of many such notices in the main Chinese cities, which suggests that a large number of executions have been carried out since the end of 1976, not only for crimes such as murder, rape, robbery and other common-law offences but also sometimes for political offences. The following are reports which mentioned political offenders.

In November 1976, various press agencies in Peking reported that travellers arriving from Changsha, the capital of the central province of Hunan, had seen official notices in the city stating that a man had been sentenced to death after defacing Hua Guofeng's name on wall posters announcing his appointment as Party Chairman.

According to travellers to Hangzhou, eight young people, including two women aged a little over twenty, were executed in February 1977 in Hangzhou (the capital of Zhejiang province). The group was said to have been accused of organizing the training of armed groups and distributing subversive literature, and to have already been criticized in 1972.[69]

In the middle of March 1977, a public notice issued by the High People's Court of Shanghai announced death sentences passed on 53 convicted criminals. Twenty-seven of them benefited from a two-year suspension of execution and 26 were ordered to be executed immediately. The 26 executed included 24 ordinary criminals and two people charged with "political crimes". One of the latter was said to have hampered criticism of the purged "gang of four" and the other to have opposed the official policy of sending "educated youth" to work in the countryside after graduation in an urban middle school.[70]

Commenting on the purge of the "gang of four", Vice-Premier Li Xiannian said in March 1977, during an interview with Sir Denis Hamilton (editor-in-chief of the *Times* Newspapers in London), that the Chinese people were demanding severe punishment, "possibly of the type that is being given to those who are being executed in the provinces".[71]

In April 1977, an official notice from Nanjing's Intermediate People's Court, posted in the streets of the city, announced sentences passed on various offenders. Three of them were sentenced to death and ordered to be executed immediately, one for common-law crimes and the other two for political offences. One of the latter two was Liu Yongda, whose case was mentioned earlier,[72] and the other,

Zhang Wenxiu, was accused of maintaining a "reactionary attitude" while serving a sentence of life imprisonment for theft and previous "bad" behaviour. According to the notice, during the period of "reform through labour", Zhang uttered "counter-revolutionary" slogans, "shamelessly supported the gang of four" and "viciously attacked the farseeing leader Chairman Hua and the CCP Central Committee, the dictatorship of the proletariat and the socialist system". The notice stated that he was an "irreclaimable obstinate counter-revolutionary element" and that the court, "in accordance with the law", had sentenced him to immediate execution. It also stated that Zhang had appealed to the High People's Court of Jiangsu province, which had confirmed the sentence, and that on 1 April 1977, he was taken bound to the place of execution to be shot. [73]

In May 1977, it was reported that eight people, all men in their twenties and thirties, had been sentenced to death in Shenyang (Liaoning province), one of them with suspension of execution for two years. A ninth offender was sentenced to life imprisonment. Among them was a 24-year-old accused of having formed his own political party, tuned in to "enemy radio" and attempted to reach the Soviet border. Another of the condemned men, aged thirty-nine, was alleged to have kept a "revisionist diary" since 1958, to have painted "counter-revolutionary" pictures and slogans and to have been a supporter of the "gang of four". Two others were accused of having disrupted rail traffic by tearing up railway track. [74]

According to travellers to the city of Anyang (Henan province) 12 alleged supporters of the "gang of four" were executed in the city on 2 August 1977. The 12 were said to have included the former Chairman of the Anyang County Revolutionary Committee, surnamed Sun, and his deputy, surnamed Li. These executions appear to have been the culmination of political unrest in the city over the previous 18 months between alleged supporters of the "gang of four" and their opponents. On 2 August, it is said that the 12 men, wearing placards round their necks, were driven in trucks to the place of execution through the crowded streets of the city. [75]

At least 23 people were executed in Kunming (Yunnan province) in September 1977, according to travellers who reported seeing six lists of condemned people in the city. They were able to read only one list which included 47 names, 23 of them listed for immediate execution, mostly for political offences. These offences included distributing counter-revolutionary leaflets and forming counter-revolutionary groups. [76]

On 28 November 1977, the official Chinese newspaper *People's Daily* called for moderation in the use of the death penalty. The article was contributed by a Ministry of Public Security theoretical study group. The authors recognized that "serious" crimes called for the death penalty but added that it is preferable to stay the execution for a period of two years to give the condemned a chance to "repent". They stressed at the same time that those who "break, smash and loot" and those who pose "a serious threat to discipline through subversion and sabotage" should be struck with a "hard blow".[77]

Despite this call for moderation, other official statements made later defended the death penalty[78] and new executions were reported in early 1978.

According to travellers who saw official Public Security posters in Hangzhou in February 1978, eight people were executed after "13 counter-revolutionary groups" had been disbanded in the city at the end of January. The eight executed were apparently the leaders of the groups which comprised no more than 32 members. One group was accused of organizing "counter-revolutionary activities with political plans" and trying to spread "propaganda aiming at undermining the socialist system". The poster stated that its leader came from a "counter-revolutionary family". In addition to receiving virtually the same charges, another group was accused also of having procured arms and forced people by armed threat to supply it with provisions.[79]

The execution of a political offender named He Chunshu was announced also in February 1978 in Canton by means of a public notice from Guangdong province High People's Court. The notice was dated 18 February 1978 and said that He Chunshu had been sentenced to death with immediate execution for printing and distributing a counter-revolutionary leaflet. The notice was remarkable in that, unlike most official announcements of convictions, it specified that He Chunshu had been sentenced to death according to Article 10, paragraph 3, of the "Act of the People's Republic of China for Punishment of Counter-Revolution", and that the sentence had been approved by the Supreme People's Court.

The notice stated that the "active counter-revolutionary He Chunshu, male, aged 45, from Nanning (Zhuang Autonomous Region of Guangxi), was a teacher at the further education school for workers and employees of Canton's light industry bureau" before his arrest.

According to the notice, He Chunshu had always had a "vicious nature" and after liberation (1949) was twice "removed from the revolutionary ranks":

Public notice from Guangdong province High People's Court, announcing the execution of a political offender, Ho Chunshu, in February 1978.

"After he became a teacher in 1956, he maintained a
reactionary attitude, deeply hated our Party and socialist
system. In 1963, he started secretly writing a large number
of counter-revolutionary articles. After the Great Proletarian
Cultural Revolution started, the criminal He frantically engaged in
counter-revolutionary sabotage activities; he wrote and
stencilled a counter-revolutionary leaflet of more than
200,000 words containing counter-revolutionary articles; using
the names of seven counter-revolutionary organizations, he
mailed it to Soviet revisionists, American imperialists,
reactionary Hong Kong newspapers, to some foreign con-
sulates and embassies in China, to institutions and press
organizations in our country, to about 10 units and people.
[In it] he viciously attacked our great leader and teacher . . .
the political campaigns launched by our Party, he attacked
the Proletarian Cultural Revolution, the dictatorship of
the proletariat; he greatly praised social-imperialism, spread
his counter-revolutionary ideas, foolishly tried to overthrow the dictatorship of the proletariat and to restore
capitalism."

The notice further stated that his "counter-revolutionary activities"
had provoked the "great anger of the large masses of the people" and
that the "dictatorship organs, under the close leadership of the party",
had finally arrested him. After his arrest, he "persistently refused to
admit his crime" . . . "His crime is very serious, the people's anger is
very great, he is a counter-revolutionary element determined to be
the enemy of the people, who obstinately refused to change. . . ."
Thus, the court sentenced him to immediate execution (sentence
approved by the Supreme People's Court) and decided that "on
18 February 1978, the criminal He Chunshu, after verification of
identity, is to be taken bound to the place of execution, where he
will be shot."

70

Notes

1 "On the Ten Major Relationships", Mao Tsetung's *Selected Works*, Vol. V, Peking, 1977, pp. 298-301 ("The Relationship between Revolution and Counter-revolution"). The extracts quoted henceforth are taken from this official translation.

2 "Exercise strict discipline, uphold justice", *Yunnan Daily* of 13 March 1978, in SWB, FE/5767, 18 March 1978.

3 See "China: The Politics of Public Security" by Tom Bowden and David S. Goodman in *Conflict Studies* No. 78, December 1976, p. 11.

4 See Cohen, op. cit., and SWB No. 418 of 30 December 1954 which gives the text of the regulations according to the NCNA of 21 December 1954.

5 See Cohen, op. cit., pp. 28-33, for more details on the difference between "detention" and "arrest".

6 Cohen, op. cit., p. 28. The Security Administration Punishment Act, 1957, provides for warning, fine and short-term detention for acts defined as "minor unlawful acts" such as disruption of public order, improper social behaviour, etc. (see Cohen, ibid., pp. 200-237).

7 In Chinese *gongren chiuchadui*; abbreviated henceforth to "workers brigades".

8 See "The Supervision and Control System of Mainland China after the Cultural Revolution" by Wen Sang in *Huang He*, No. 3, 25 April 1977.

9 Many groups or "factions" were formed throughout China during the Cultural Revolution. In each city and institution there were generally two rival factions: the "rebels" who identified with an ultra-leftist line and the "conservatives" who were closer to the interests of conservative cadres inside the Party.

10 Yang confessed to having said "three antis": anti-Party, anti-Mao Tsetung and anti-socialism.

11 Wen Sang, op. cit., *Huang He*, No. 3, 25 April 1977.

12 See Chapter I, p. 12.

13 Article by Tadashi Ito (former Kyodo correspondent in Peking), Kyodo in English, 1 September 1977.

14 See Chapter I, p. 22.

15 The organization of such "study clases" is generally an indication that one or several of the participants are in trouble and have to remould their way of thinking. The practice is derived from one of Mao's sayings that the "reactionaries" have to "sit in socialist classrooms" in order to change their viewpoint.

16 The "reception stations"—in Chinese *shou rong zhan*—are normally transit detention places for vagrants, people who travel without permits or who do not have proper identification papers, or for offenders who are transferred from one place to another. Detention is generally short in reception stations as they are only clearing houses.

17 Act of the PRC For Reform Through Labour, adopted in 1954; see Chapter III, p. 75, for details on this law.

18 See p. 54, the remark of a Shanghai High Court judge.

19 See in Appendix 4, p. 158, the detailed description of a particular case during the "one-strike three-anti" campaign.

20 See p. 47.

21 See Chapter I, p. 21, a directive from Mao in 1968. Similar directives are usually given in all campaigns.

22 See p. 54, the statement of a judge from Shanghai.

23 "An Interview with Chinese Legal Officials" by Gerd Ruge, in *China Quarterly*, No. 61, March 1975, pp. 118-126.

24 These criticisms were made by lawyers and judges in 1957 during the "Hundred Flowers" movement (see Chapter I, p. 17).

25 Wu Te-feng's address "On the preservation of the Socialist Legal System", January 1958, in *Bulletin of the International Commission of Jurists*, No. 8, December 1958, pp. 7-8.

26 Ruge, op. cit., p. 118.

27 Richard P. Brown, "Present-day Law in the People's Republic of China" in *American Bar Association Journal*, Vol. 61, April 1975, p. 476.

28 Heilongjiang provincial radio service of 13 August 1977 on the "conference of representatives of advanced units on the judicial front to learn from Taching and Tachai from 4th to 12th August in Harbin", in SWB, FE/5593 of 19 August 1977.

29 SWB, FE/5669, 17 November 1977.

30 "The Law in China: Impressions of a Visit" by Christian Broda, in *Europaische Rundschau*, No. 2/77, p. 46.

31 Brown, op. cit., p. 477. See also Ruge, op. cit., p. 123.

32 Martin Garbus, "The Political-Legal System in Red China" in *New York Law Journal*, Vol. 177, No. 25, 4 February 1977, p.4.

33 ibid.

34 Brown, op. cit., p. 477.

35 Ruge, op. cit., p. 125.

36 Garbus, op. cit., p. 5.

37 Decision of the Standing Committee of the National People's Congress of the PRC Relating to Cases the Hearing of which is to be Conducted Non-publicly, 8 May 1956, in Cohen, op. cit., p. 442.

38 See, for example, in Chapter I the cases of Zheng Chaolin (p. 15), Hu Feng (p. 15), Lin Xiling (p. 18) and other cases in Appendices.

39 See "Public trial rallies in People's China" in *Bulletin of the International Commission of Jurists*, September 1968, pp. 25-29. The article mentions in particular a televised public trial held in Peking on 28 January 1968 involving 11 defendants, three of whom were apparently charged with political offences. The sentences announced ranged from seven years' imprisonment to the death penalty.

40 Ruge, op. cit., pp. 120-121.

41 See p. 67, for more details on this case.

42 See Cohen, op. cit., pp. 20-21, for more details about "informal" penalties.

43 About "struggle" sessions, see Chapter IV, p. 128.

44 There is little official information about appeals. A Chinese judge interviewed by Edgar Snow in 1960 said of both criminal and political cases that "only about five per cent of the verdicts" were appealed against and "not over twenty per cent [of these]" were reversed. Snow, op. cit., p. 348.

45 See Chapter I, p. 6.

46 Cohen, op. cit., p. 41.

47 See Chapter I, p. 18.

48 An amnesty was also proclaimed on this occasion, see Chapter V, p. 146.

49 See Cohen, op. cit., p. 268, and below, Chapter V, p. 147.

50 See an example in Chapter I, pp. 21-22.

51 See Li Yizhe's poster "Concerning Socialist Democracy and Legal System" in *The Revolution is Dead, Long Live the Revolution*, Hong Kong, 1976, p. 274. According to a radio broadcast from Canton on 21 March 1978, the official *Nanfang Ribao* (Southern Daily) stated that the review of "wrong verdicts" which started in 1970 was "greatly restricted and could not even be done in a perfunctory way" due to the influence of the "gang of four". (SWB, FE/5783, 8 April 1978.)

52 See an example in Chapter I, p. 24.

53 SWB, FE/5690/B11/3, 12 December 1977.

54 See Reuter and Agence France Presse from Peking, 14 March 1978.

55 See Chapter III, p. 77, and Chapter IV, p. 119.

56 See Chapter I, pp. 4-5.

57 Article 3 of the Act of the PRC for Punishment of Corruption, 1952.

58 Article 9, ibid.

59 Article 3 of the Provisional Statute for Punishment of Crimes that Endanger the State Currency, 1951.

60 Brown, op. cit., p. 477.

61 "Lectures" (September 1957), in Cohen, op. cit., p. 538.

62 See Shao-chuang Leng, *Justice in Communist China*, Oceana Publications, New York, 1967, p. 167.

63 Peter Griffiths, Reuter, Tientsin, 7 August 1975.

64 "Justice in China" by Sven-Erik Larsson in *Dagens Nyheter* of 6 November 1977.

65 Interview with Professor Han Yu-tung, NCNA in English, 21 February 1978.

66 See "Les grands procès publics en Chine populaire", *Bulletin de la Comission Internationale des Juristes*, September 1968. According to this article, about 70 people were sentenced to death and executed between August 1967 and May 1968, and at least 70 other death sentences were pronounced during the same period with suspension of execution for two years.

67 See p. 45, about this campaign.

68 See one case in Chapter I, p. 26.

69 See Reuter and Agence France Presse from Peking, 12 March 1977.

70 Reuter and Agence France Presse, Peking, 17 March 1977.

71 London *Sunday Times* of 27 March 1977.

72 See Chapter I, p. 26.

73 See "Der Volkszorn ist sehr gross", *Der Spiegel*, 22 August 1977.

74 Reuter and Agence France Presse, Peking, 23 May 1977.

75 *Far Eastern Economic Review*, 19 August 1977.

76 Reuter, Peking, 31 October 1977.

77 *Le Monde* of 30 November 1977.

78 See Agence France Presse, Peking, 4 December 1977 and NCNA of 21 February 1978.

79 Agence France Presse, Peking, 26 February 1978.

Corrective Labour and Penal Policy

> "Our Government policy regarding counter-revolutionaries
> consists of repression combined with clemency."
> (Zhou Enlai's report to the National People's Congress,
> 23 September 1954.)[1]

The penal policy of the People's Republic of China places more
emphasis on the "reform" of offenders than on their physical confinement for a fixed period of time. Such reform is carried out by
compelling both criminal and political offenders to engage in
productive labour while undergoing political re-education. This policy
is based on the principle that offenders can be and should be "transformed into new people" through work—that is, that their consciousness should be changed to conform to the political and economic
standards of society. When this policy was made law in 1954, official
comments indicated that it was intended as a means of controlling
offenders which would eventually result in a reduction of crime. It
was also seen as a more humane treatment of offenders than enforced
idleness. In addition, the prisoners' compulsory labour also served
another purpose: making penal institutions economically self-
sufficient and contributing to the economic development of the
country.

As previously noted,[2] not all political offenders are formally
sentenced by a court after being convicted of a "crime"; some
offenders receive "administrative" penalties imposed by a simple
administrative or police order. Moreover, convicted offenders sentenced to terms of "imprisonment" lasting from two to twenty years
generally carry out their sentence by "reform through labour", not
necessarily in a prison. Both convicted and unconvicted political
offenders can be held in the following penal establishments:

— detention centers, which are used mainly for offenders not yet
  convicted who are held for investigation, but also for convicted
  offenders sentenced to short terms of imprisonment (up to two
  years);
— corrective centers for juvenile offenders (reformatories holding
  only juvenile delinquents);

- corrective labour farms, where the following categories of people can be held: convicted prisoners sentenced (by a court) to "reform through labour"; non-convicted offenders "assigned" (by administrative order) to "rehabilitation through labour"; juvenile delinquents (when they cannot be placed in a reformatory); and "free-workers" (offenders who are "retained" in a penal establishment at the expiration of their term of imprisonment);[3]
- corrective labour camps—generally temporary camps set up to build railways, roads, factories, bridges, dams, dikes, etc., or existing in mining areas. They usually hold mainly convicted prisoners sentenced to "reform through labour", but "rehabilitation through labour" offenders may sometimes be sent to them;
- prisons, which include factories and workshops. They can hold "reform through labour" prisoners, "rehabilitation through labour" offenders, juvenile delinquents, "free-workers", and also "major" offenders sentenced to life imprisonment or to the death penalty with suspension of execution, who usually do not work.

This chapter examines the main provisions of the legislation on corrective labour; the next describes certain aspects of their practical application. The main legal documents relevant to corrective labour mentioned in this chapter are:

- Act of the People's Republic of China for Reform Through Labour (1954);
- Decision of the State Council of the PRC Relating to Problems of Rehabilitation Through Labour (1957);
- Provisional Measures of the PRC for Control of Counter-revolutionaries (1952, amended 1956).

Principles

The principles and methods of China's penal policy are outlined in the Act of the PRC for Reform Through Labour, adopted by the Government Administration Council on 26 August 1954.[4] Although this law was enacted nearly five years after the establishment of the PRC, the penal system it lays down had been shaped and applied long before then. The first experiments made by the CCP leaders in controlling political opponents through imprisonment date from the period when communist bases were established in Jiangxi province (1927-34) and methods for reforming prisoners were evolved in the communist bases in northern China (Yan'an) between 1935 and 1945.[5] The policies developed in Yan'an are quite similar to those applied after 1949.

When the law on "reform through labour" was adopted in 1954, the Minister of Public Security, Luo Ruiqing, stated in an official commentary[6] that the law had been in preparation for a long time and had been the subject of numerous discussions, including some with Soviet jurists. He stressed that there were three elements of equal importance in the penal system: (1) the carrying out of punishment, (2) "production"[7] through compulsory labour, (3) the practice of political thought reform.

Commenting on past experience in handling offenders, the Minister said: "Facts prove that the policy of reform through labour practised towards criminals is able to bring criminal elements to reform themselves during the period they labour, this is why it is an efficient means of suppressing reaction and of destroying all crimes and transgressions at the roots."[8] He also commented on the productive output of offenders' compulsory labour: "All this production work is not only profitable for the development of the various construction enterprises of the country, but it spares the nation large expenses and constitutes for it a fixed source of wealth."[9] The Minister estimated that revenues from reform through labour for the following year would be such that "at the end of 1955 the total of profits and expenses for the whole country would be more or less balanced."[10]

Another official commentary published in the *People's Daily*[11] when the law was promulgated on 7 September 1954 gave the percentage of prisoners who at that time were already participating in production work as 83 per cent of all those detained in the whole country. They were engaged in agricultural and industrial work, forestry, in building roads and railways and in other major construction projects. This article stressed that, unlike the general population's participation in productive labour, the offenders' work was compulsory, unpaid and, furthermore, done under strict control.

Corrective labour legislation

(i) Labour-reform

The Act for Reform Through Labour is one of the most detailed laws of the PRC. It includes 77 articles which are divided into seven sections: (1) general principles, (2) organs of "reform through labour", (3) labour and ideological reform, (4) the production of "reform through labour", (5) the system for supervising offenders, (6) the control and administration committee, (7) rewards and punishments.

The purpose of the law is defined in its first Article as being "to punish all counter-revolutionary and other criminal offenders and to compel them to reform themselves through labour and become new persons".

According to Article 3, convicted offenders shall, according to the nature of their crimes and the seriousness of the punishment, be held under different régimes in prisons and "reform through labour corrective brigades";[12] offenders not yet convicted shall be held in detention centers; juvenile offenders shall receive "reform through education" in corrective centers specifically for them.[13]

Different types of régime apply to different categories of convicted offenders. Those whose cases are officially considered "major" and who are sentenced to long-term imprisonment are usually held in prisons and subjected to a "strict régime of control and discipline". The law provides that sentenced offenders held in prisons may be put in isolation (solitary confinement) "when necessary".[14] Major offenders are discriminated against in other ways. Article 37 provides that the following shall not be imprisoned: offenders with mental, serious contagious or other kinds of serious illness; pregnant women; women whose imprisonment is due to begin six months or less after giving birth. However, those who have been convicted of major political or criminal offences are specifically excluded from this provision by the law. Moreover, while Article 60 provides that offenders who are seriously ill and who *need* to obtain a guarantor and seek medical treatment outside the prison shall be allowed to do so with the approval of the relevant authorities, offenders whose crimes are "heinous" are excluded from this provision. It is probable, therefore, that major offenders who become seriously ill may be denied proper medical treatment if this cannot be provided where they are detained or through transfers to special hospitals. The law, however, does not include any provision for special medical treatment in such cases. It simply states in a general way that the organs of reform through labour, depending on their size, shall establish dispensaries, hospitals and other such institutions for medical treatment and shall have the necessary medical equipment.[15]

Major convicted offenders generally do not work at the beginning of their imprisonment (sometimes for several years). If their behaviour is judged satisfactory after a period of intense compulsory education, they may be put to work in the place where they are imprisoned.

The majority of convicted offenders (that is, those sentenced to terms ranging from two to twenty years' imprisonment) are assigned to work in "reform through labour corrective brigades", or—more briefly—"labour reform brigades". The Law on Reform Through Labour prescribes the following work schedule:

"The time for actual labour for offenders generally shall be fixed at nine to ten hours each day. With seasonal production it may not exceed twelve hours. The time for sleep generally shall be fixed at eight hours. The time for study may be fixed in accordance with concrete circumstances, but it shall not be permissible to average less than one hour a day. Sleep and study periods for juvenile offenders shall be appropriately extended. Offenders who do not participate in labour should have one to two hours a day of outdoor activities.

"A day of rest for offenders shall generally be fixed at once every fortnight, for juvenile offenders once every week."[16]

To make offenders work for nine to ten or twelve hours a day may seem a contradiction of the reformist principles according to which the law was drawn up. However, as previously pointed out, the official commentaries on the law emphasise labour and production.[17] Compulsory labour is the main method of "reforming" prisoners—the test whereby they will prove that they have reformed—whereas "education" is used only as a complementary method. In this respect, the law stipulates that attention must be paid to the cultivation of the offenders' production skills and "labour habits", as well as to the full use of the technical skills they may have (Article 27). "Competition may be used" to increase production efficiency and promote a positive attitude towards work (Article 23).

Another article of the law indicates that the purpose of combining labour with political education is "to make compulsory labour gradually approach voluntary work" (Article 25). Despite this, there are severe punishments for prisoners who do not work as prescribed. According to the section of the law concerned with rewards and punishments, the seven meritorious acts for which an offender may receive a reward include three concerning labour and production (Article 68). On the other hand, offenders may be punished for simple "lack of care" of tools or machines, or for "deliberately working slowly" (Article 69). More important, Article 71 provides that "open resistance to work despite repeated education" is one of the "crimes" for which an offender may receive an additional sentence.

The power to approve rewards and punishments lies with the responsible officials of the penal institutions—that is, the Public Security officers appointed to manage them—and it is on their recommendations regarding prisoners' behaviour that the people's courts will consider reducing or increasing sentences.[18]

The overall production of labour-reform institutions is planned and controlled by the economic agencies of the state administration (at local or national level), with the co-operation of the police and judicial bodies as regards its management.[19] Article 30 of the law provides that labour-reform production must serve the cause of the state's economic construction and be included in the national economic plan. According to Article 35, the Ministry of Public Security may move prisoners from one region to another, according to the number of prisoners in one region or the state's economic needs. Minor or temporary transfers may also be made locally for the same purpose with the Ministry's permission. In practice, this provision results in greater separation of prisoners from their families since visits—which are guaranteed by Article 56—become a remote prospect if a prisoner is transferred hundreds of miles away from home.

Ideological or "thought" reform is carried out through study sessions which, according to the law, must last for no less than one hour a day. Section 3 of the law contains precise instructions on the way to "re-educate" offenders. According to Article 26, it is to be done through the systematic use of "collective classes, individual conversations, assigned study of documents, discussions and other such methods", which are aimed at educating offenders "about admitting their guilt and observing the law, about current political events, about labour and production and about culture". This provision is compulsory. The second part of Article 26 is optional: it states that offenders may be organized in sporting and cultural activities and in examination of their lives, labour and study. The organization of such activities is, therefore, apparently left to the discretion of the penal institution officials. However, this is not the case as regards the control of prisoners' daily life and behaviour which, according to Article 29, must be scrutinized and recorded closely:

> "In order to examine the circumstances of the reform of offenders a card file system shall be established for them. Moreover, there shall be special persons to administer this system and to record *at any time*[20] the circumstances of the offenders' observance of discipline and their behaviour with respect to labour and study. Evaluation shall be made periodically."[21]

Such periodical evaluations are probably recorded in prisoners' individual dossiers since, according to the law, such dossiers are begun whenever offenders are taken into custody; they record biographical data and details regarding health, culture, family situation and special abilities, as well as information on the crime, punishment and the court which passed sentence (Article 41).

In order to encourage reform, the law includes a system of rewards and punishments.[22] The ultimate reward provided for offenders who show they have reformed and repented is reduction of sentence or release. However, the law is imprecise about how such a decision is taken and about how great a reduction of sentence may be granted. It simply states that this depends on the "degree" of reform and repentance. Wide discretionary powers are, therefore, given to the local authorities.

The law is similarly vague about increase of sentences and disciplinary measures. Article 46, for instance, stipulates that implements of restraint (that is, shackles, fetters, etc.) may, with the approval of responsible officials, be used on offenders when there is a "possibility" of their escaping, being violent or engaging in "other dangerous acts". Although it specifies that the restraints must be removed as soon as "the above circumstances are eliminated", there is no further clarification of what constitutes the "possibility" of violence or a dangerous act. Similarly, Article 59 provides that an offender's right to receive visits, parcels and mail and to send letters may be limited or completely suspended in "special circumstances", but the law does not specify what these circumstances are. According to Article 72, lack of "activism in labour" coupled with repeated violation of prison rules are circumstances which may lead to the extension of offenders' terms of imprisonment if "facts prove that they still have not reformed and that there is a real possibility that they will continue to endanger the security of society after release."

This provision, therefore, makes release even on expiry of sentence conditional on prisoners' "good" behaviour, the assessment of which, again, is largely left to the local authorities. Supplementary regulations about release—dealt with later[23]—were promulgated separately in 1954 to specify the conditions for the release of convicted offenders.

The law on Reform Through Labour also provides that conditional release (parole) can be granted to two categories of offenders: those suffering from serious illnesses requiring treatment outside prison (except, however, for major offenders), and those who are at least 55 years old or physically disabled, serving a term of up to five years' imprisonment, and no longer a "danger to society"; the period of conditional release counts as part of the offender's term of imprisonment (Article 60).

Various protections and rights are guaranteed to offenders by the law. The most important protection is included in Article 5, which categorically prohibits "cruel treatment and torture". Article 47 provides that guards and other officials shall be held criminally responsible for any "erroneous use of weapons which constitutes a criminal act" (guards may use weapons as a last resort when offenders engage in specific violent acts and disobey orders to stop). According to Article 34, arrangements must be made for safety rules at work, and suitable care must be given to a male prisoner or to his family if he is maimed or killed due to an accident at work or a natural calamity. As stated earlier, offenders who are ill (unless they are "major" offenders) are also allowed to seek medical treatment outside their place of detention in certain cases. If a prisoner dies, the law provides that a legal-medical inquest shall be carried out by the local people's court and that the family shall be notified (Article 54). Female offenders are not allowed to take their children to prison with them, but the law provides that, if they are unable to make private arrangements for the children's care, the civil affairs departments of the administration shall entrust the children to the care of local residents, orphanages or nurseries, with all necessary expenses paid out of social relief funds (Article 39).

The law also contains provisions for prisoners' daily life, their rights to visits and correspondence, which will be examined later.

When the Law on Reform Through Labour was promulgated in 1954, it covered all the types of detention there were for the reform of offenders. The regulation on rehabilitation through labour which was adopted three years later institutionalized a new type of corrective labour: "rehabilitation through labour".

(ii) Rehabilitation through labour

Unlike "reform through labour", "rehabilitation through labour" was not conceived as a criminal punishment, but as an "administrative punishment" for those who are not legally considered "criminal".

The stated aims of the Decision on Rehabilitation Through Labour[24] adopted in August 1957 are:

> ". . . to reform into self-supporting new persons those persons with the capacity to labour who loaf, who violate law and discipline or who do not engage in proper employment and . . . further to preserve public order and to benefit socialist construction."[25]

Rehabilitation through labour is further defined in the Decision as "a measure of a coercive nature for carrying out the education and reform of persons receiving it. It is also a method of arranging for their getting employment." (Article 2) According to an official press commentary, "the method of rehabilitation through labour embodies the socialist principle that he who does not labour does not eat."[26]

The coercive aspect of rehabilitation through labour which "benefited" socialist construction was the institutionalization of compulsory labour for people who, according to Chinese legal standards, had either committed no "crime", or whose "crime" was too minor to warrant their prosecution under criminal law. As can be seen from the quotations above, the law avoids the terms "arrest", "offender" and "confinement" for those affected by rehabilitation through labour. In the official terminology, they are "summoned" by the police and not "arrested", they "receive" rehabilitation instead of being "confined" and, unlike convicted offenders, at the end of their term of "rehabilitation" they are not "released" but simply "dismissed".

This law was drawn up primarily to control vagrants, minor offenders, troublemakers who did not work properly or who refused to comply with work assignments and people who were unemployed because they had been expelled from their place of work for a breach of discipline or other reasons.[27] However, for the sake of the campaign against "rightists", launched in June 1957, the law included a paragraph directly affecting political offenders. The majority of "rightists" were dismissed from their work when they were given a "rightist's hat" and came, therefore, within the terms of the following article:

(Article 1) "The following kinds of persons shall be provided shelter and their rehabilitation through labour shall be carried out:

(1) . . .

(2) "Those counter-revolutionaries and anti-socialist reactionaries who, because their crimes are minor, are not pursued for criminal responsibility, who receive the sanction of expulsion from an organ, organization, enterprise, school or other such unit and who are without a way of earning a livelihood."

Commentaries in the official press stressed the positive aspects of the law in reforming and providing employment for "bad elements", and treated it as indicative of the state's concern and sense of responsibility for these people.[28] However, the commentators did not speak of those who had lost their jobs and come under the jurisdiction of this law solely for exercising their constitutional right to freedom of speech.

According to the Decision on Rehabilitation Through Labour, rehabilitation through labour differs from reform through labour in three main ways. First, those assigned to rehabilitation through labour are paid (with various deductions) a salary fixed according to the nature of their work and output.[29] Second, no specific length of time is fixed for rehabilitation: it may be terminated at any time if those concerned "behave well".[30] This deliberate loophole may have been due to the wish to stress the "non-criminal" character of rehabilitation through labour, but it left the door open to abuses by the local authorities since, according to the law, those in charge of rehabilitation through labour are responsible for approving the discharge of people who have been punished in this way. In 1961, however, a special regulation fixed the maximum period of rehabilitation at three years. The text of this legislation is not available to Amnesty International but is has been widely reported that there is a three-year time limit.[31] It is reported also, however, that failure to reform during these three years may result in an extension of the punishment for a maximum of one or two years and that in a case of persistent "bad" behaviour, a person's status may be changed (probably by a court) to that of "reform through labour" offender.

The third difference from reform through labour is that rehabilitation through labour is approved by administrative bodies and not by the courts; it does not, therefore, require judicial or procuratorial investigation or any other legal process and the offenders concerned have no legal claim against it. The law also allows an application for imposition of rehabilitation through labour to be made by various civil bodies or by individuals:

> "If a person must be rehabilitated through labour, the application for rehabilitation through labour must be made by a civil affairs or a public security department; by the organ, organization, enterprise, school, or other such unit in which he is located; or by the head of his family or his guardian. The application shall be submitted to the people's council of the province, autonomous region, or city directly under the central authority, or to an organ that has been authorized by them, for approval."[32]

Apart from these differences, the methods of labour-rehabilitation are rather similar to those of labour-reform; production is also combined with political education and the rules of discipline are the same. Furthermore, offenders punished by "labour-rehabilitation" are assigned to work either in special labour-rehabilitation farms or in penal establishments, which they have, in both cases, no right to leave. A former prisoner, Bao Ruowang, stated that, while he was held in a corrective labour farm in the north of China in 1960, though "labour-rehabilitation" offenders "were technically considered citizens", they did the same work as convicted prisoners and ate the same rations.[33] He cited the reply of a warder to "*laojiao*" (labour-rehabilitation) offenders who had complained about their treatment: ". . . *Laojiao* people are here to expiate their mistakes by hard work . . . as far as we are concerned *laojiao* and *laogai* (labour reform) are the same."[34]

It seems, however, that at the time the law was adopted, experiments were made to organize rehabilitation through labour in villages for resident offenders who qualified for this sanction, and who could live with their families during the time of rehabilitation.[35] This, however, did not apply to the majority of those assigned to rehabilitation through labour for political reasons, who were, in the main, urban intellectuals or civil servants and were sent to work either in corrective settlements specially created for "rehabilitation through labour" offenders or in already existing penal establishments.[36]

(iii) Control

As noted earlier, "control" is one of the punishments by which an offender may be compelled to engage in corrective labour. Although the offender is formally sentenced to this punishment for a fixed period of time, "control" is generally carried out in society: after sentencing, the offender is usually sent back to his or her original place of work or residence to work under "control". This is provided for in Article 10 of the Law on Reform Through Labour, which also stipulates that the sentence be enforced by the local state administration or department where the offender originally worked.

However, some offenders thus sentenced have also had to serve their sentences in work units other than the one to which they originally belonged.

The Provisional Measures for Control of Counter-revolutionaries, adopted in 1952, were designed solely for political offenders.[37] They provided that control was to be sanctioned either by a court or by a Public Security body[38] —that is, with or without a court judgment— and that the term of control could be increased if offenders did not carry out their obligations under the sentence of control.[39] The main obligations are listed in Article 5 of the law as follows:

(1) to observe the government's control provisions;
(2) to engage in proper employment and labour actively for production;
(3) on discovering it, immediately to report the counter-revolutionary activity of others.

In fact, violation of the control provisions could mean, among other things, failure to ask permission not to go to work, failure to report to the cadres at stated times, missing a political study session, or not working hard enough. The sentence could, therefore, be increased for simple misconduct. The law also made denunciation compulsory (Article 5, paragraph 3, above) and encouraged it as one of the ways by which punishment might be reduced or terminated. [40]

In 1956, however, this law was modified in two main points by a Decision of the Standing Committee of the National People's Congress.[41] The Standing Committee decided that henceforth control could be imposed only by a court judgment, and that the decision to reduce or increase the term of control also belonged to the courts. Moreover, the decision to increase the sentence was henceforth to be based on the discovery of a new offence and not on simple violation of the control provisions. This Decision, therefore, made "control" a formal punishment and softened the most severe provision of the original law. Furthermore, the Standing Committee Decision referred to the control of "counter-revolutionaries and other criminals", thus going beyond the 1952 law by including ordinary criminal offenders among those who should be controlled and implying that political offenders would be sentenced to control only after being convicted of a "crime".

Control is officially regarded as a mild punishment because it generally does not involve isolation from society and is imposed only for a relatively short period (up to three years, according to the law). Nevertheless, it has many of the features of more severe criminal punishments, including compulsory labour and deprivation of political and civil rights. According to the 1952 law on control, "controlled elements" are deprived in particular of the rights to vote and stand for election, to work in the administration, to join the armed forces and "people's organizations", and of all the constitutional rights to freedom of speech, association, correspondence, etc.[42]

Categories of imprisonment

Convicted or unconvicted political offenders are sent to a variety of places of detention. Various categories of offenders are often held in the same place of detention, but each category has its own régime. The penal institutions are officially defined as "instruments of the people's democratic dictatorship".[43] They are run by the Public Security bodies at the level at which they are established (for example, a *county* detention center is run by the county Public Security bureau) and armed guards are supplied by the Public Security armed units. Some penal institutions are under the direct control of the central Government (through the Ministry of Public Security). [44]

Huiyang county (Guangdong province) Detention Center

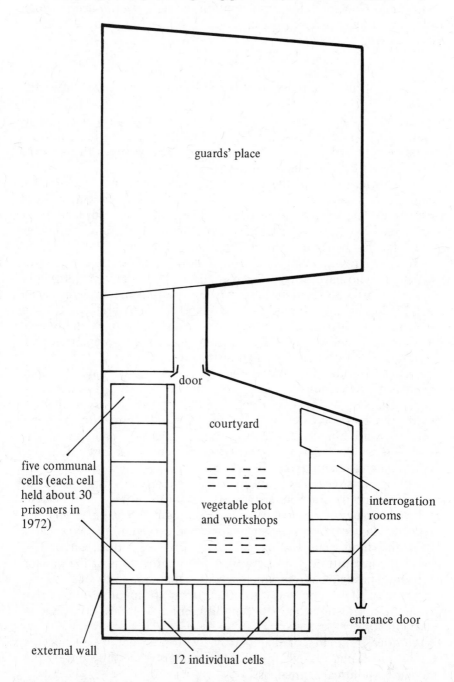

guards' place

door

courtyard

five communal cells (each cell held about 30 prisoners in 1972)

vegetable plot and workshops

interrogation rooms

entrance door

external wall

12 individual cells

(i) Detention Centers

The usual Chinese term for detention center is *kanshousuo* (which literally means "place to watch-guard"), but places of detention are also referred to as *juliusuo* (*juliu* means "detention").

In accordance with the Law on Reform Through Labour, detention centers are established at all administrative levels,[45] from the county—the basic administrative level in the countryside—up to the national level where they are controlled directly by the central Government. They vary greatly in size, depending on the level at which they are established. Some in country areas are built to hold about a hundred people (see diagram, p. 85), whereas those in the provinces or big cities may hold several thousand.

Under the terms of the law, the officials in charge of detention centers are a director and one or two deputy-directors. One cadre is usually in charge of political education and discipline for a group of prisoners. He is called *guanjiaoyuan*, "instructor", and supervises the detainees' behaviour during detention.

The law provides that detention centers are to be used mainly for offenders who have not yet been tried, but that they may also hold convicted offenders sentenced to two years' imprisonment or less when it is "inconvenient" to send them to "labour-reform brigades".[46] The meaning of "inconvenient" is not specified, but presumably this measure is aimed at reducing the number of unnecessary transfers, thus easing the strain on the administration.

Convicted offenders and those not yet convicted have different régimes in detention centers. According to the law, they must be kept separate, and whereas convicted offenders are compelled to work, those whose cases have not yet been judged may do so only if this does not hinder the investigation or trial.[47] Furthermore, the law specifies that offenders not yet convicted whose cases are major must be kept in solitary confinement.

Former prisoners have reported that, whatever the seriousness of their case, political offenders are often held in solitary confinement for varying periods at the beginning of their detention. It is also reported that detainees as yet unconvicted receive only two meals a day, the food generally being insufficient to nourish anyone of average constitution. This is contrary to the provisions of the Law on Reform Through Labour which specifies that standards of food and clothing shall be imposed "according to uniform provisions"—that is, with no distinction between different categories of offenders (Article 50).

Another frequent complaint made by former detainees concerns the overcrowding of cells in detention centers, especially during the numerous political campaigns.

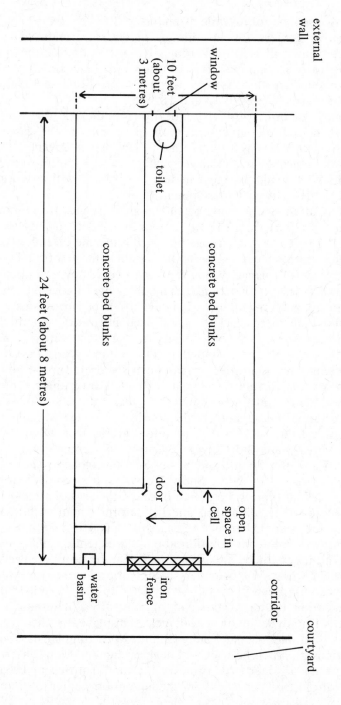

Diagram of a communal cell which held about 30 prisoners in 1972:
Huiyang county (Guangdong province) Detention Center

(ii) Corrective centers for juvenile offenders

The corrective centers for juvenile offenders (reformatories) are listed in the Law on Reform Through Labour as one of the four institutions for carrying out the reform of offenders. They are designed to conduct the "reform through education" of juvenile offenders between the ages of 13 and 18.[48]

The term "reform through education" indicates that more emphasis is placed on education than on labour in the case of juvenile offenders. This is stressed in the law, which specifies that they shall be educated in the new morality, in basic culture and in production skills, while engaging in light work, and with attention being paid to their physical development.[49]

Like adult offenders, juvenile offenders are sentenced to criminal punishment. A report from the Ministry of Public Security, issued in February 1958, stated that altogether 4,500 juvenile offenders had already been so sentenced.[50] The report said that nine new (or rebuilt) reformatories with a capacity of over 5,000 would soon be opened in nine major cities. At that time, the majority of sentenced juvenile offenders were held together with adult offenders in prisons and labour camps due to the lack of specialized institutions for them.

The reformatories' lack of capacity to accommodate juvenile offenders seems to have continued in the ensuing years. In 1961, two of Peking's reformatories were reportedly overcrowded and a decision was taken to transfer juvenile offenders from these centers to two prison-farms outside Peking: the *Qinghe* state farm (east of Tianjin) and the *Tuanhe* state farm (south of Peking) where adult offenders were held also. The Peking reformatories from which they were transferred were the "Juvenile Corrective Center" (*shaonian guanjiaosuo*) and the "Work and Study School" (*gongdu xuexiao*). The latter was visited by Edgar Snow in 1960 and, according to his report, held at that time 185 children between the ages of 10 and 15. He reported also that Peking had another reform school with about 100 juvenile delinquents between the ages of 15 and 18.[51]

There is little recent information about the detention of juvenile offenders, although there are occasionally imprecise references to teenagers held with adult offenders in detention centers. One such case involved a fourteen-year-old boy reported to have been held in a Peking detention center at the end of May 1974. The case was mentioned without details in a wall poster displayed in the city in June 1974 by a man named Chung Chun-te who complained about the conditions in which he was held in the same detention center.[52] Another former prisoner told Amnesty International that in 1969 a thirteen-year-old boy was held in the detention center of Baoan county, Guangdong province, after receiving a three-year sentence. The boy had been arrested, it was said, for shouting "reactionary" slogans such as "long live Liu Shaoqi" and refusing to stop despite his father's admonitions.

Reports from the 1960s indicate that juvenile delinquents are held in better physical conditions than adult offenders, although they are subjected to a similar discipline. In the *Qinghe* farm mentioned above, juvenile offenders were said to spend half of the working day studying and half in doing manual labour. They received nearly the same amount of food as adult prisoners working full-time and it was of better quality. They were given pocket-money according to the type and amount of work they did and they received a "resettlement" sum when they were discharged from the farm. They were not deprived of political rights,[53] as were adult convicted prisoners. If their crime was serious enough to warrant a conviction, they were sentenced to "reform through labour" when they reached the age of 18.

Some of this has been confirmed by a recent official report: according to an article in the Swedish newspaper *Dagens Nyheter* of 6 November 1977,[54] reporting an interview with a judge from Shanghai High Court, a teenager under 18 who commits a crime is sent for three years to a reformatory where half the time is spent in study and the other half in doing manual labour. According to the report, juvenile delinquents whose crimes are of an "unusually serious nature" may be transferred from a reformatory to prison at the age of 18.

(iii) Rehabilitation through labour groups

The Chinese term *laodong jiaoyang*—more commonly used in its abbreviated form, *laojiao*—can be translated as "rehabilitation through labour", "re-education through labour" or, more briefly, "labour re-education".

Those who are given this "administrative" punishment are sent either to farms holding only labour-rehabilitation offenders or to penal institutions (prison-factories, camps, farms) holding other categories of offenders, in which case they work and live separately from the latter.

Offenders assigned to labour-rehabilitation (or "re-education") generally have a slightly better diet and, at least according to the law, more privileges than convicted prisoners sentenced to reform through labour: in particular, better shopping facilities, the possibility of voicing complaints about their treatment and, if they show "good" behaviour, of being granted brief leave to visit relatives; they also receive a salary. However, in spite of the distinction made by the law between rehabilitation and reform through labour, and although the former is imposed on people who have not been tried and convicted, it is generally reported that the work required of and the discipline imposed on offenders in these two categories are similar. Both categories have to work very hard for an average of eight to ten hours a day and the stigma attached to both punishments is said to be practically the same.[55]

Moreover, there is evidence that many political offenders assigned to labour-rehabilitation after the "anti-rightist" campaign of 1957 were, like convicted offenders, sent to faraway regions to do pioneer work. According to former prisoners, "rightists" from Peking, Shanghai, Canton and other cities were sent mainly to the northeast (formerly Manchuria), the northern part of which is called the "North Great Wilderness", *beidakuang*, because of its harsh climate and sparse population. One complex of labour-reform farms in Heilongjiang (the northern-most province on the Soviet border) is known to have held labour-rehabilitation inmates in the 1960s; the complex is known as the *Xingkaihu*[56] and was said to be under the control of Peking's Public Security Bureau. The 850th branch-farm of the *Xingkaihu* complex held labour-rehabilitation offenders. Ding Ling, a well-known woman writer who was branded as a "rightist" in 1957, is reported to have spent a year there before being transferred to another, unknown, place.[57]

At the time of the Cultural Revolution (1966-68), public complaints were said to have been voiced about the system of labour-rehabilitation, complaints supported in some areas even by local officials of the Public Security. These complaints apparently stressed the unfairness of a system whereby people not legally considered criminals were kept in detention. It is alleged that it was then discovered that groups of "rightists" and other labour-rehabilitation offenders had been "forgotten" in some labour-rehabilitation farms and camps since the early 1960s. According to report, as a result of public complaints and pressure from some Public Security personnel, many of these farms and camps were closed down at that period, particularly in the provinces of the central-south of China.

However, new labour-rehabilitation farms and camps are reported to have been opened from 1969 onwards to accommodate people who were again given this punishment during the waves of arrest between 1968 and 1970. Due to the severity shown towards political offenders after the Cultural Revolution, even "minor" political offenders were generally sentenced to reform through labour after 1968 and the majority of those assigned to rehabilitation through labour were, according to reports, petty offenders and common-law criminals.

(iv) Reform through labour brigades

Reform through labour in Chinese is *laodong gaizao*, abbreviated to *laogai* (labour-reform).

Labour-reform prisoners serve their sentences in "reform through labour corrective brigades" (abbreviated henceforth to "labour-reform brigades"). These penal brigades may constitute a part or the whole of a prison-factory, farm or camp; they may also constitute a temporary (or mobile) camp set up to build factories, railways, bridges, etc. The labour-reform brigades are known internally by numbers but these are not made public. Prisoners usually refer to their places of detention by the names of the farms, factories or areas where they are established.

Labour-reform prisoners are often transferred from one camp to another according to the state's "economic needs". Those who receive long sentences (generally 10 years or more) are particularly liable to be sent to do pioneer work in sparsely populated areas, often very far from their own homes. There is evidence that even when they remain in their home provinces, labour-reform prisoners are given the hardest work to do for the sake of the country's economy and are used as a mobile, unpaid labour force. It is not uncommon, for instance, for them to have to build their own camp and bring under cultivation previously uncultivated land, and for the camp later to be transformed into a state farm or one managed by mixed labour, while the prisoners are either transferred somewhere else or assigned to the hardest work in the camp. This seems to have been the case with a large camp in the north of Guangdong province called *Yingde* — the name of the county where it is situated.

The *Yingde* camp was established in 1952 for labour-reform prisoners who built their own houses and cleared the land. The camp was then divided into five brigades (*dadui*) each comprising between 500 and 1,000 prisoners, who worked in an agricultural unit and in several mines, including, it is said, a plutonium mine. Over the years, the camp became economically successful. It expanded over a very large area, and a tea plantation producing the "*Yingde* Red Tea" was developed. In 1967, in addition to agricultural brigades and the tea plantation, the camp had a granite and a chalk quarry, a repair plant for agricultural machines, a mechanical plant and a school specializing in the cultivation of tea. It reportedly had then more than 10,000 workers there, including convicted prisoners, labour-rehabilitation offenders, "free-workers" and ordinary workers. According to various sources, in 1969 part of the camp became a May 7th Cadre School,[58] while at the end of 1970 the tea plantation was gradually transformed into a state farm for "educated youths" (urban high school graduates). When these changes occurred, some of the prisoners were transferred to another part of the area covered by the camp, where they again had to do pioneer work.

According to the testimony of a former prisoner, another labour camp in Lianping county, Guangdong province, was built by prisoners between 1971 and 1973. More than 2,000 prisoners were there in 1974, including political and criminal offenders. The first prisoners sent to this county in 1971 were transferred from over-crowded labour camps in neighbouring counties. They had to build everything themselves, starting with rudimentary shelters, then going on to erect the camp's external wall which was made of stone and three metres high (see diagram on p. 93). During the period of construction, the prisoners were divided into one building middle-brigade (*zhongdui*) and three agricultural middle-brigades. Food was limited somewhat until agricultural production had reached a sufficient level, since normally prisoners eat food which, for the most part, they have produced. However, during the period of construction, funds were allocated to the camp to purchase grain, oil and other necessary products, equivalent to 10 *yuan* per month per person. [59] According to information received by Amnesty International, the prisoners were at first pleased to be transferred to this area, but their enthusiasm was quickly dampened by the disadvantages of pioneering: hard work in conditions generally inferior to those they had known previously.

The prisons, farms and camps which hold various categories of offenders have separate "brigades" for labour-reform (convicted) prisoners, labour-rehabilitation offenders and "free-workers"; but in the "labour-reform brigades" criminal and political prisoners usually live and work together. However, one case of political and criminal convicts being kept separate has been reported to Amnesty International: between 1968 and 1970, political prisoners held in a camp in Zeng Cheng county (Guangdong province) were reportedly kept apart from criminal prisoners. At that period, political prisoners were in the majority in this camp and were, apparently, openly discriminated against, often being denied their rights and allowed fewer privileges than criminal prisoners.

(v) Prisons

Prisons are generally in cities and provincial capitals. According to the law, they are intended to hold mainly major offenders sentenced to long-term imprisonment, over whom a strict control can be better

Labour-reform camp in Lianping county (Guangdong province) built in 1971

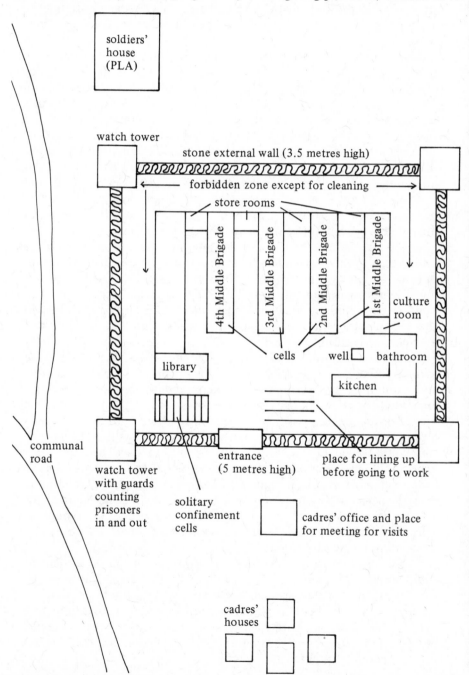

maintained in prison than in labour-reform brigades. In fact, most prisons are factories and therefore include other types of offenders—labour-reform or labour-rehabilitation offenders, as well as "free-workers".

Major convicted offenders are separated from other offenders in prison and subjected to a different régime. They are in general not allowed to work until they are considered to have progressed in "ideological reform". The prohibition on work is regarded both as a punishment and a security measure to prevent contacts with other prisoners and the circulation of information about their cases. Most of their time is spent in study and "self-examination" sessions, during which they have to review again and again their past and present attitudes. Their reform program includes repeated confessions and self-denunciations, and denunciations of other people. Like other offenders, major offenders are also reminded that their sentences may be reduced if they prove that they have reformed and repented.

Offenders submitted to this régime are usually dangerous or recidivist criminal offenders and important or recidivist political offenders. In the north of China, for instance, Fushun prison (Liaoning province) included until 1975[60] a special center for high-ranking Guomindang officials, most of whom had been arrested in the 1950s. The center was called the "War Criminal Control Center of Shenyang Military District" and several years before had held Japanese war criminals and former Manchu officials, including the former emperor, Pu Yi. The rest of this prison consisted of factories and buildings for ordinary prisoners and is reported to have expanded considerably over the years.[61]

The presence of prisoners under special surveillance has been reported in other regions, sometimes in labour camps like the *Yingde* camp mentioned above. This camp is said to have held in 1967 major political and criminal offenders sentenced to life imprisonment or a suspended death sentence. According to one report, they lived in a special compound surrounded by barbed wire and guarded by soldiers. Some were in solitary confinement, others in communal cells. They did not work, were allowed out of their cells only for fresh air and were said to wear fetters.

According to a former detainee, in 1968 the prison of Sechen He (Shiquanhe, the capital of Ngari administrative area, Autonomous Region of Tibet) had a special "isolation" section where up to 30 or 40 prisoners were kept in solitary confinement, five of whom had been arrested in 1968 for "high treason". This special section could be seen from the courtyard of the general prison but "ordinary" prisoners could not enter it.

Location of places of detention

No official statistics are available on the number and location of places of detention in the PRC; it is therefore difficult to give any precise picture of their distribution.

"Labour-reform brigades"[62] are especially difficult to locate because, unlike prisons and detention centers, they are not a type of "establishment" as such, but may form part of a prison, camp or farm. Moreover, little recent information is available on labour camps established in the 1950s or 1960s. One study published in France in 1958, the *Livre blanc sur le travail forcé dans la République populaire de Chine*, includes a map giving the location of 297 places of detention reported to have existed in the 1950s.[63] However, the book gives no information about most of them and it is unclear whether they represent detention centers, prisons, farms or camps. Some former prisoners have supplied specific information about prisons and camps in published accounts, notably Bao Ruowang (Jean Pasqualini) in *Prisoner of Mao*,[64] Allyn and Adele Rickett in *Prisoners of Liberation*,[65] and Duan Kewen in a series of articles in *Shijie Ribao (World Journal)*.[66]

The difficulty of locating labour-reform brigades is due to certain features of the labour-reform system concerning the assignment of prisoners:

— transfers of prisoners occur frequently and camps or farms known to have held prisoners at one period may later be handed over to civilians;
— prisoners may be assigned to institutions which employ civilians too and are therefore not necessarily identified as penal institutions;
— prisoners may be sent to mobile or temporary camps, which are closed down once the construction project for which they have been established is completed.

However, an indication of the distribution of penal institutions is given by the 1954 Law on Reform Through Labour. It specifies the administrative level at which each type of institution can be established: detention centers in rural counties and districts, cities, provinces or at national level, controlled by the central Government; and prisons, labour-reform brigades and reformatories for juvenile offenders in provinces and cities. This means that each province may have several prisons and labour camps and numerous detention centers. The information available to Amnesty International generally confirms that there are a large number of detention centers, prisons and camps spread throughout the country. The Provincial Public Security Departments control the penal institutions established in their respective provinces. In addition, some large labour-reform farms or camps, in sparsely populated border regions, are reported to be under the direct control of the national Ministry of Public Security.

As previously stated, the law provides that prisoners may be transferred from their home provinces to other regions, according to the state's economic needs or to the number of prisoners in any one region.[67] There is apparently no restriction on this procedure: prisoners from any part of China may be transferred to a faraway region with a different climate and language from that of their native place, and with practically no prospect of receiving visits from their relatives because of the distance. Prisoners in some pioneer zones are said to have been allowed, before 1960, to request permission for their families to join them as settlers, but after 1960 this privilege was apparently granted only to "free-workers" (ex-prisoners who are retained or placed in the camps after release). The change is attributed to the increased frequency of prisoner transfers from one place to another and to the lack of proper housing accommodation in the camps.

With some exceptions—in particular those provided by law for "major" offenders—criminal and political offenders are mixed in prisons and labour camps.

The north-east of China is one of the pioneer zones where large numbers of prisoners have been sent over the years. According to a former prisoner who was held in the north-east from 1954 to 1972, there are more than a hundred state farms in that region, 60 to 70 per cent of which are penal institutions. Another long-term prisoner who worked from 1953 to 1954 in Jilin province, in Changchun *Jinjianbao* (labour-reform) Brigade No. 1 (a brick factory where there were then about 3,000 prisoners), estimated that there were more than 30 similar brigades in the province.[68]

Although these estimates have not been corroborated by other sources, there are generally reported to be numerous corrective labour settlements in the north-east. In Heilongjiang province, a complex of labour-reform farms was created between 1953 and 1955 in the east of the province, between Mishan and Raohe, near the Oussouri River which runs along the Soviet border up to Lake Xingkai (Xingkaihu). One of these farms, the *Xingkaihu* farm, is named after the nearby lake. In 1960 this farm was divided into nine branch-farms spread among some 60 villages. Part of the farm was closed down in 1964 as a result of the Sino-Soviet dispute and some of the prisoners were transferred to the *Paicheng* camp in Jilin province. (Prisoners near the border in other parts of Heilongjiang were reported to have all been transferred at that time to the "second defence line" and soldiers replaced them in the farms along the border.)

The *Xingkaihu* farm alone is said to have held some 40,000 convicted prisoners, labour-rehabilitation offenders, juvenile delinquents and "free-workers", plus a large number of their dependants. It was then a vast complex, having its own tractor-servicing stations, repair shops, electric power plants, a paper-making factory, a sugar refinery, a milk-processing plant and a canning factory. The soil in the area is very rich and fertile, but the climate is extremely hard. As in other parts of Heilongjiang, the average temperature is about −40°C between November and March, but work is compulsory for prisoners unless there is a strong wind. In addition, part of this area consists of marshlands, infested by mosquitoes in the summer and difficult to drain and cultivate.

Another complex of labour-reform farms exists in the west of Heilongjiang province. The farms were opened in the mid-1950s near Zhalaiteqi and Haila'er, in what was then the third district of Inner Mongolia: Hulunbeier special district (*meng*). This district of Inner Mongolia has now been integrated into Heilongjiang province.[69]

In Zhalaiteqi, the *Baoanzhao* farm was opened up in 1954 by prisoners coming from Shanghai and from the provinces of Jiangsu, Zhejiang, Fujien, etc. (generally from the east coast of China). This farm is said to cover an area of 600,000 *mou* (about 40,000 ha.) and to contain about 40,000 prisoners, both criminal and political (it is not known whether the figure includes "free-workers"). It is divided into four branch-farms each holding about 10,000 prisoners. During the four months of the year when there is no frost, the prisoners work in the fields, growing grain crops, potatoes, sugar beet, etc. For the rest of the year they work in repair shops, canning and paper-making factories and a sugar refinery, or at building roads and farms, digging trenches, and so on.

The existence of labour-reform farms and factories in Inner Mongolia was mentioned in 1958 in the official newspaper of Inner Mongolia.[70] The paper criticized waste and bad management in the penal institutions of the region, mentioning in particular the *Baoanzhao* farm, three farms in Baotou and a brick- and tile-making factory in Huhehaote (the capital of Inner Mongolia). According to other reports, a labour-reform farm called *Zhangyi* was opened in 1960 in Inner Mongolia to accommodate prisoners working in mines near Baotou after the mines were turned over to the Ministry of Mines. Prisoners at this farm worked to transform the arid desert soil into fertile patches of land capable of producing food crops. The Baotou iron and steel factory was built in part by prisoners between 1954 and 1958. It was said still to hold prisoners in the early 1970s, as did the Anshan iron and steel factory in Liaoning province (in the north-east).

Temporary camps are set up also to build railways, roads, dams and other construction projects. The stretch of the Peking-Erlian railway line (at the Mongolian border) which crosses Inner Mongolia was built by prisoners between 1951 and 1954. They were housed in tents and lived and worked in hard conditions. The temperature in this area remains far below zero°C for over five months of the year. It is reported that about 8,000 prisoners from Guangdong province were sent to this area in groups of up to 1,500; other groups were sent from east coast provinces to work on the railway and to do other construction work. Some of them were later assigned to building another major railway line between Baotou (Inner Mongolia) and Lanzhou (Gansu province). Large numbers of prisoners are said to have worked in the 1950s also at building the Zhongqing-Chengdu line in Sichuan province[71] and in the 1960s on railway lines between Lanzhou (Gansu province) and the Tsaidam area (Golmo, Ke'ermu in Qinghai province).

There is little precise information on any border region of the PRC except the north-east, although various sources mention the existence of large labour-reform settlements in the Uighur Autonomous Region of Xinjiang (north-west) and in Yunnan province (south). One Xinjiang camp is said to be under direct government control, guarded by soldiers and holding only male offenders, the majority of whom are said to be "historical counter-revolutionaries" (mainly former low-ranking officials of the Guomindang). The *Livre blanc* (see above, p. 95) reports that towards the end of 1954, prisoners from Shandong province were transferred to the Koko Nor (in Qinghai province), Xinjiang and Tibet.[72] Exiles have reported the existence of labour camps in Tibet near Lakes Nagtsang and Pongong (north-north-west of Lhasa) for mining chromium ore, and of small labour-reform "groups" in the Lhokha administrative area of Tibet, in particular in Tsethang (*Zidang*, south of Lhasa).[73] Prisons of various sizes holding both ordinary criminal and political offenders are also said to exist in the main Tibetan cities, in particular *Dapchi* and *Sangyip* prisons in Lhasa (the first is said to be Prison No. 1 of the Autonomous Region of Tibet), *Karkang* prison in Shigatse and *Sechen Ho* prison (*Shiquanhe*) in Ngari Administrative area. *Sangyip* prison is alleged to have held some 1,800 prisoners in 1972, most of them Tibetan political offenders, whose work was stone-quarrying and brick-making, blacksmithing, building construction and carpentry.

In the east and center of China, labour camps have, over the years, been located in practically all the provinces, but detailed, up-to-date information is too scanty to give an over-all picture of their present distribution. The examples given below have therefore been limited to a few large cities and regions on which Amnesty International has detailed or cross-checked information. It must be emphasized that all labour-reform farms, prison-factories and camps described by prisoners at one time or another held both criminal and political offenders and that recent reports indicate that a large number of labour-reform establishments exist throughout the country.

Among the earliest accounts, that given in the *Livre blanc* of the organization of camps in Shandong province in 1955 is noteworthy. [74] A reorganization of the administration of the camps is reported to have been carried out in the province in 1954/55, resulting in the creation of six labour-reform "general corps" directly under the jurisdiction of the provincial government. According to this report, the second and fourth "general corps" were located in Jinan (the capital of the province), holding 5,000 and 15,000 offenders respectively, and the first "general corps" was established in Huimin (north of the province) and was said to hold about 40,000 detainees.

The Public Security Bureau of Peking itself directly controls several corrective labour farms, camps and prison-factories, some of which are outside the administrative area under its jurisdiction. The largest ones are the *Xingkaihu* farm in Heilongjiang province (mentioned earlier) and the *Qinghe* farm, east of Tianjin. The *Qinghe* farm was started in 1950 with some 1,200 prisoners from Peking. An official document stated in 1954 that 5,384 people had been released from this farm during the previous four years, [75] which suggests that the prisoner population had rapidly increased since the opening of the farm in 1950. In the 1960s the farm is said to have had some 10,000 convicted prisoners, labour-rehabilitation offenders, "free-workers" and their families; it was divided into three branch-farms and nine agricultural units covering a large area (some 16,000 m wide by 30,000 m long). Branch-farm No. 1 was a maximum discipline camp holding only convicted offenders, mainly troublesome or "dangerous" prisoners. Unlike the *Xingkaihu* farm, however, the *Qinghe* farm held no prisoners serving life sentences. Branch-farm No. 2 held only labour-rehabilitation offenders and branch-farm No. 3 had mixed labour, including juvenile delinquents. The nine agricultural units were established during the Great Leap Forward (1958) and consequently were designated by numbers, starting with 58. One of them, Camp 585, is said to have had the worst living conditions of the whole farm because it held old or sick prisoners, generally unfit to achieve a normal level of production.[76]

In addition to the *Xingkaihu* and *Qinghe* farms, ten smaller labour-reform farms and factories outside Peking were, in the mid 1960s, identified as being under the jurisdiction of the city's Public Security Bureau. Most of them had a mixed labour force of convicted prisoners, labour-rehabilitation offenders and "free-workers". It is not known whether they are still used as penal institutions. In addition, Peking had two prisons. One of them, Peking Prison No. 2, was a prison-factory to the north of the capital. In the early 1960s it held some 2,000 labour-rehabilitation offenders and "free-workers", plus a handful of convicted offenders. Known to outsiders as the "New Capital Engineering Works", it produced mainly radiators and machine parts. Amnesty International has no recent information on this prison.

Another prison in the capital—Peking Prison No. 1— has occasionally been visited by Western journalists. According to various reports, between 1956 and 1957 it held more than 1,200 men and 40 women serving sentences of between 3 and 10 years, plus some serving life imprisonment, and 100 ex-prisoners ("free-workers");[77] in 1958, it was reported to have 1,500 prisoners, two-thirds of whom were political offenders, including 10 under suspended death sentence;[78] in 1960, the prison had 1,800 prisoners, of whom 40 per cent were political offenders, more than 100 were female offenders and 60 were under suspended death sentence.[79] In 1963-64, the prison population was reported to consist of about 2,000 prisoners (including some 300 women), plus 500 "free-workers", and an unknown number of offenders undergoing labour-rehabilitation. The prison then included five factories (producing stockings, towels and industrial equipment), a translators' brigade, a hospital, and even a theatrical company made up of artist-prisoners and "free-workers" which periodically performed in the camps under the Peking jurisdiction.

Peking Prison No. 1 is situated in the former premises of Peking's Model Prison in the south of the capital. A detention house known as the *nansuo* (southern compound), attached to it, has reportedly held at times as many as 4,000 detainees. It included in the mid-1960s a separate wing for scientists and highly-qualified technicians, most of them serving long sentences.

In 1972, foreigners visited prisons in Shenyang (Liaoning province) and Tianjin. At Shenyang there were 2,000 prisoners (political and criminal offenders)[80] and at Tianjin more than 1,100 prisoners (half of them political offenders), with over 100 female offenders. Shanghai city has one large prison which in 1977 was officially said to have some 2,700 convicted prisoners (including 200 women); about 10 per cent of the 2,700 were said to be political offenders. In the entire administrative area under the jurisdiction of Shanghai Public Security Bureau there are reported to be at least 18 detention centers and three labour-reform farms.[81] In Canton, two prisons are said to be under the city's jurisdiction, and it is reported that the provincial administration of Guangdong controls one prison (Guangdong Province Prison No. 1). Amnesty International has also received information about five labour-reform farms or camps in different counties of Guangdong province and there are said to be many more labour camps in the province. One refugee has alleged that Guangdong province has a prison designated "Prison No. 1 of the PRC", also known as the "Shaoguan Food Processing Factory".

There are numerous detention centers throughout the country, the smaller ones being established in rural counties. In major cities they appear to be distributed in the following way: one small detention center in each municipal district and one larger one at the city level, which functions as a "head office" for all the others. In addition, some provinces have "receiving centers" (shourongsuo) which function as transit centers for detainees and clearing houses for vagrants or people arrested for lack of proper identification papers.[82]

Notes

1 *People's Daily* of 23 September 1954, translated in *Livre blanc sur le travail forcé dans la République populaire de Chine*, Commission internationale contre le Régime concentrationnaire, Centre international d'Edition et de Documentation, Paris, 1958, Vol II, p. 27.

2 See the section on "penalties" in Chapter II, pp. 57-59.

3 On "free-workers", see Chapter V, pp. 143-146.

4 "Act of the PRC for Reform Through Labour", adopted on 26 August 1954 by the 222nd Political Conference of the Government Administrative Council (GAC), promulgated by the GAC on 7 September 1954, published in *Zhongyang Renmin Zhengfu Faling Huipien 1954*, Peking, 1955, pp. 33-43. Translated in Cohen, op. cit., A. Blaustein, op. cit., *Livre blanc sur le travail forcé dans la République populaire de Chine* (referred to henceforth as *Livre blanc*).

5 See Patricia Griffin, "Prison Management in the Kiangsi and Yenan periods" in *China Quarterly*, No. 58, April/June 1974, pp. 310-331.

6 Luo Ruiqing (Lo Jui-ching)'s Report to the 222nd Political Conference of the Government Administrative Council on 26 August 1954, in *Livre blanc*, p. 329.

7 That is, the agricultural and industrial production of the penal establishments, which results from the offenders' obligatory work.

8 Luo Ruiqing's report, *Livre blanc*, p. 328.

9 ibid., p. 328.

10 ibid., p. 329.

11 "Apply to the end the policy of reforming criminals through labour", *People's Daily* of 7 September 1954, translated in *Livre blanc*, pp. 333-336.

12 This term refers to any working unit where prisoners sentenced to "reform through labour" can be sent to carry out their sentence. In fact, it can be a part of a prison, of a labour camp or farm. Henceforth the abbreviation "labour-reform brigade" is used for it.

13 See pp. 86-94, for details on the various categories of imprisonment.

14 Act for Reform Through Labour, Article 14.

15 ibid., Article 53.

16 ibid., Article 52, translation taken from Cohen, op. cit., pp. 592-593.

17 See p. 75.

18 Articles 70, 71, 72.

19 Article 31.

20 Emphasis added.

21 Translation taken from Cohen, op. cit., p. 591.

22 Briefly mentioned earlier, p. 77; see also Chapter IV, pp. 119-121 for more details.

23 See Chapter V, pp. 141-143.

24 The full title is: "Decision of the State Council of the PRC Relating to Problems of Rehabilitation Through Labour" (approved 1 August 1957, promulgated 3 August 1957), in *Zhonghua Renmin Gongheguo Fagui Huipian* (Collection of Laws and Regulations of the People's Republic of China), Vol. 6, p. 243; translated in Cohen, op. cit., pp. 249-250. Abbreviated henceforth to Decision.

25 Introductory paragraph of the Decision (see note 24).

26 *People's Daily*, 4 August 1957, translated in Cohen, op. cit., p. 255.

27 Decision, Article 1, paragraphs 1, 3 and 4.

28 *People's Daily*, 4 August 1954.

29 Decision, Article 2.

30 Decision, Article 4.

31 See Cohen, op. cit., p. 240; and "The Control System in Mainland China after the Cultural Revolution" by Wen Sang in *Huang He*, No. 3, 25 April 1977.

32 Decision, Article 3, translation taken from Cohen, op. cit., p. 250.

33 Bao Ruowang, *Prisoner of Mao*, Coward, McCann, New York, 1973, p. 208.

34 ibid., p. 209.

35 See the example given by the *Kansu Daily* of 20 July 1958, in Cohen, op. cit., pp. 250-254.

36 See pp. 89-90, for more details.

37 See Chapter I, pp. 5-6, Article 3 of the Provisional Measures of the PRC for Control of Counter-revolutionaries.

38 Provisional Measures, Article 11.

39 ibid., Article 7.

40 ibid., Article 8, paragraph 3.

41 "Decision of the Standing Committee of the NPC of the PRC Relating to Control of Counter-revolutionaries in all Cases Being Decided Upon by Judgment of a People's Court", passed on 16 November 1956, in *Zhonghua Renmin Gongheguo Fagui Xuanji*, Peking, 1957, p. 263; see translation in Cohen, op. cit., p. 279.

42 Provisional Measures, Article 4.

43 Act for Reform Through Labour, Article 2.

44 ibid., Articles 6, 11, 15, 19, 23 and 44.

45 ibid., Article 11.

46 ibid., Article 8.

47 ibid., Article 9.

48 ibid., Articles 3 and 21.

49 ibid., Article 22.

50 "Report of the Ministry of Public Security Relating to the Work of Preparing the Establishment of Corrective Centers for Juvenile Offenders", 21 February 1958, in *Zhongyang Renmin Zhengfu Fagui Huipian*, Vol. 7, 1958, p. 215; translated in Cohen, op. cit., p. 595.

51 Snow, op. cit., p. 366.

52 See report from Agence France Presse in Peking, by René Flipo, 25 June 1974.

53 For instance, the right to join the "people's organization", which in their case would be the Communist Youth League.

54 Larsson, op. cit.

55 See Martin K. White, *Small Groups and Political Rituals in China*, University of California Press, 1974, pp. 194-210, and Wen Sang, op. cit., p. 7.

56 See Bao Ruowang, op. cit., pp. 194-199.

57 Ding Ling was reported in early 1978 to be free and living in Shanxi province with her family (see *Far Eastern Economic Review*, 3 March 1978).

58 The "May 7th Cadre Schools", which are usually farms, were opened after the Cultural Revolution for cadres who had to engage in manual labour, generally for short periods, not, however, as a punishment. These "schools" therefore should not be mistaken for penal institutions.

59 Ten *yuan* is equivalent to slightly more than 5 US dollars.

60 "War Criminals" and former Guomindang officials were released by a special amnesty in 1975. See *China Pictorial* No. 7, 1975 and Reuter of 23 December 1975.

61 Duan Kewen, "The Narration of a War Criminal", daily articles in *Shijie Ribao* (a Chinese-language paper published in New York) in 1976 and 1977: article of 30 October 1976.

62 For convenience the term "labour camp" will be used instead of "labour-reform brigade".

63 *Livre blanc*, Vol. I, p. 300.

64 Bao Ruowang, op. cit.

65 Allyn and Adele Rickett, *Prisoners of Liberation*, Anchor Press/Doubleday, New York, 1973.

66 Duan Kewen, op. cit.

67 See above, p. 78.

68 Duan Kewen, op. cit., 22 October 1976.

69 Inner Mongolia was split into three main parts during the Cultural Revolution and the northern part was integrated in Heilongjiang province.

70 *Inner Mongolia Daily (Neimonggu Ribao)* of 28 February 1958, quoted in *Saturne* No. 18, April-May 1958.

71 *Livre blanc*, Vol. II, pp. 258, 265 and 282.

72 *Livre blanc*, Vol. II, p. 457.

73 *Tibetan Bulletin*, Vol. IX, No. 3, Sept-Oct 1977.

74 *Livre blanc*, Vol. II pp. 455-465.

75 Luo Ruiqing's report to the Government Administrative Council's 222nd political conference, 26 August 1954, see *Livre blanc*, Vol. II, p. 331.

76 See Bao Ruowang (Pasqualini), op. cit., p. 245.

77 See report from Richard Hughes in *Far Eastern Economic Review* of 15 April 1977.

78 See *"Chine, fer de lance du Communisme"*, a series of articles by Fernand Moulier in *Le Figaro*, 12-18 September 1958.

79 Snow, op. cit., p. 358.

80 See article by Ingmar Lindmarker in *Svenska Dagbladet*, 19 May 1972.

81 See letter from a "Shanghai resident" in *Far Eastern Economic Review*, 8 April 1977.

82 For detailed information about the "receiving centers", see the "Control System of Mainland China after the Cultural Revolution" in *Huang He*, No. 3, 25 April 1977.

Treatment and Conditions

Conditions for prisoners in Chinese penal institutions have varied greatly at different periods, according to changes in the country's economic or political situation. There are also, at any given time, important regional variations in the treatment of prisoners, and each type of imprisonment has its own particular régime. The conditions described in this chapter, therefore, are not meant to give an over-all picture of the situation of prisoners in the whole of the country at any given moment.

However, several aspects of detention conditions have, over the years, been the subject of constant complaints by prisoners, in particular the system of punishment, the inadequacy of food and the lack of proper medical care, which make it difficult for prisoners to comply with the requirements of corrective labour. The hardship caused by forced labour is regarded by the authorities as an integral part of the prisoners' reform. Prisoners are expected to accept hard work and suffering without complaint as an indication that they are trying to make up for their past crimes or mistakes. If, on the other hand, they complain, are slow at work or are judged to have a "bad" attitude, they are classified as "resisting reform" and are punished in various ways, the ultimate punishment being an increase of sentence.

Work

Prisoners in labour-reform farms and prison-factories are organized on a military basis. A farm or factory of medium size usually includes a battalion of prisoners or, in Chinese, a "brigade" (*dadui*), which is further divided into companies, platoons, groups, etc.

In very large labour-reform farms, the "brigade" itself is only a sub-division of the farm. For example, the *Baoanzhao* labour-reform farm (*nongchang*) in Heilongjiang province is divided into four branch-farms (*fen chang*) each with about 10,000 prisoners and workers. Each branch-farm is subdivided into 10 to 12 "units" (*danwei*), with varying numbers of prisoners (from 500 to more than 1,000). In the *Baoanzhao* farm, a brigade either corresponds to a large "unit" or includes several small "units". In 1970, for instance, one of the farm's brigades included four small units each consisting of more than 500 people, and each unit was subdivided into three "middle-brigades" (*zhongdui*). One middle-brigade was in turn broken into "groups" (*xiaozu*), each composed of about a dozen prisoners.

The basic level for the allocation of work in this farm is the middle-brigade (*zhongdui*). It has one chief (*zhongduizhang*) who is an official from the camp administration and one or more other cadres in charge of the maintenance, work and supervision of prisoners. In addition, one middle-brigade prisoner (the *tongjiyuan*)[1] is appointed to take charge of production and each group (*xiaozu*) has also one leader chosen by the cadres from among the prisoners.

In the morning, after the middle-brigade chief has allocated work to the group leaders, the *tongjiyuan* tells them what work has to be done on an area of field in a certain amount of time. The group leaders in turn instruct the prisoners and urge them to carry out the assigned work during the day, whether or not it exceeds the normal working schedule. The prisoners are exhorted to work hard and not to talk to each other. Everyone's attitude at work will be examined in the evening during the "study session" and those who worked slowly will be criticized by the group leader, who also invites the prisoners to report on and criticize each other. The group leader will in turn be criticized by the cadres if the group's work record is generally inadequate. As will be seen later, insufficient work is considered an indication of a "bad" attitude and leads to punishment.

In the *Baoanzhao* farm the daily schedule varies according to the season. Work in winter is different from other seasons', as the soil is frozen for about five months of the year. There are periods of intensely hard work, such as the spring, when there is ploughing and sowing to be done, and the late summer and autumn, the harvest time, when prisoners work an average of 12 hours a day. Generally they get up half-an-hour earlier in summer than in winter. The normal working schedule in the spring/summer in the early 1970s has been described to Amnesty International in this way:

6.00 a.m.	get up and have breakfast
6.30 a.m.	assembly and departure for work in the fields
12.00 a.m.	lunch and rest in the fields (if it is not a "busy" period, prisoners can rest until 2 p.m.)
1.00 p.m.	resume work
6.00 p.m.	(if work is finished) assemble and return to the camp
7.00 to	(depending on time of return to the camp) dinner in
8.00 p.m.	the cells. Then some free time.
9.00 p.m.	"study", which normally takes place in groups (*xiaozu*).

During periods of intensive production, instead of the normal "study" by groups, the whole middle-brigade is gathered for meetings aimed at "encouraging production" and "warning the bad elements". In addition, special meetings may be called at any time to criticize or "struggle against" a prisoner. The duration of study therefore varies according to the problems being reviewed.

Prisoners have one day of rest every fortnight.

In the autumn, prisoners work at threshing after the harvest, then in the granary stocking grain, which is later transferred to the public grain store. Next comes a period when they go out to swampy areas to cut grass which is used to make paper. In winter some units work in the farm factories and workshops, while others labour outside on construction work.

The summer working schedule of the *Baoanzhao* farm is not exceptional. In a Tianjin (*Tientsin*) prison, the routine schedule for prisoners in 1972 was officially described to foreign visitors as follows:

6.00 a.m. (in winter)	
5.30 a.m. (in summer)	get up
6.30 a.m.	breakfast
7.30 a.m.	work
12.00 a.m.	lunch
1.00 p.m.	resume work
5.30 p.m.	dinner
6.30 to 8.30 p.m.	study
9.00 p.m.	lights out
	The prison officials said that the prisoners had one day of rest a week.

Refugees described the official working schedule of *Sangyip* prison (in Lhasa, Autonomous Region of Tibet) as being, in 1972, about eight hours a day, and it was usually followed. However, the prisoners doing factory and handicraft work were, according to report, made to work four hours' overtime for which they received an extra ration of 7 ounces (200 grammes) of *tsampa* (the standard Tibetan diet, made of barley) and a cup of black tea after work.

Prisoners in the main Shanghai prison were officially reported in 1977 to be working eight hours a day and to be doing two hours of political study in the evening.

The Law on Reform Through Labour[2] stipulates that the time for offenders' "actual labour" shall generally be fixed at nine to ten hours each day and that at periods of "seasonal production", it may not exceed 12 hours a day. It specifies also that offenders shall generally have one day of rest every fortnight, and juvenile offenders one day a week (Article 52).

In practice, prisoners' testimonies and interviews with officials indicate that the "normal" working day in prison-factories and farms does vary from 8 to 12 hours depending on production needs, and that prisoners normally have one day of rest either every week or every fortnight. In the north, outdoor work can be shortened in winter and completely stopped if there is a wind, when the temperature drops below $-20^0 C$.

However, on labour-reform farms, the prisoners' recorded working hours generally do not include the time taken to reach the fields and return to the camp, which may be several miles away from the place of work. Moreover, the prisoners' legal right to have one day of rest every fortnight is often denied during periods of intensive production.

Longer hours of work are usually imposed on prisoners in the following circumstances: times of seasonal production (on farms); during special production drives (mainly in prison-factories); periods when there is competition over production throughout the country; when there is an important construction project (roads, railways, dams, dikes, building bridges or factories, dredging river beds, etc.) to be completed. There have sometimes been such intensive production drives that prisoners have worked practically non-stop for several days, or more than 12 hours a day for weeks or months.[3] For example, on the 850th farm of *Xingkaihu* (Heilongjiang) from the late 1950s to the early 1960s, political offenders who were grouped together in a "rightists' company" are said to have worked an average of 14 to 16 hours a day and, during the Great Leap Forward (1958-59), to have worked day and night for periods of ten days at a stretch with virtually no rest. Mainly because of overwork, but also because of malnutrition, by the end of 1960, about 20 of the 100 people who had originally formed the company, had reportedly fallen ill and died. The members of this company were all former government civil servants from Peking who had been labelled "rightists" in 1957 and assigned to "rehabilitation through labour" on this farm. Amnesty International has received reports that intellectuals sent to corrective labour farms in the early 1960s were often singled out to do the dirtiest and most tiring work and were addressed frequently by the offensive term "stinking intellectual"[4] —humiliation was considered necessary for the reform of educated people.

The energy needed for an average of 8 to 12 hours' manual work a day, plus one or two hours of "study" in the evening, could only come from a high food ration, enabling prisoners to remain in good health and still do the work expected of them. This, however, they do not get, and prisoners serving long sentences who do not receive extra support from their families or who do not show a sufficiently good political attitude may easily be caught in a vicious circle: their work output declines with their health and their food rations are reduced accordingly.

Food

The Law on Reform Through Labour states that standards of food in penal institutions shall be imposed according to "uniform provisions", and that the administration shall strive for variety and improvement in prisoners' diet and pay attention to the eating habits of offenders from national minorities.[5]

The provisions fixing prisoners' food rations have not been published, but prisoners have reported that various rationing norms came into force in the late 1950s, with distinctions made according to the prisoners' categories and the work they do. Generally, the three following categories get different rations:

— Offenders who do not work (mainly in detention centers).
— Offenders who work. In this category different rations are fixed according to individual output and the type of work done. Individual rations are decided on by the authorities in the penal institutions, usually after mutual and self evaluation[6] by the prisoners themselves, on the basis of the authorized maximum and minimum ration.
— Offenders on a punishment régime.

In considering prisoners' diet, it should be noted that dairy products are rarely used in China, and that fruit and sweets are usually taken between meals. Oil and pork fat is used for cooking and sugar is included in some meat or fish dishes.

Prisoners receive no more than a basic diet (including cereals, vegetables, oil and only occasionally fish or meat) in which the lack of protein is not compensated for by quantity.

Cereals are the main element in the diet. Depending on the region and camp they are in, prisoners may receive corn (usually made into bread), or rice (*dami*), or gruels of maize, millet (*xiaomi*) or sorghum (*kaoliang*). A man aged between 30 and 40 undertaking 8 to 12 hours' manual labour a day generally needs between 50 and 60 *catties*[7] of cereals a month. The majority of prisoners have almost always received less than this amount and hunger is a feature of their lives.

Convicted offenders who work full-time as a rule receive three meals a day, with more or less the same type of food at each meal.

In 1958, rations for prison-factories and labour-reform farms were reported to be fixed at a maximum of 64 *catties* and a minimum of 33 *catties* per month.[8] The average food rations for prisoners in the north of China were described in 1964 as:

- 44 *catties* for labourers doing heavy work
- 35 to 42 *catties* for labourers doing medium work
- 32 to 34 *catties* for labourers doing light work
- 30 *catties* for sick and convalescent prisoners; those seriously ill received one meal of wheat-flour bread a day as additional nourishment.

Prisoners under temporary punishment régimes in the 1960s are reported to have received the following reduced rations:

- normal work with reduced rations: about 7 ounces of cereals (slightly less than half a *catty*)[9] a day for a maximum of a week
- solitary confinement: about 7 ounces of corn-mush a day for the first 8 to 15 days with a gradual increase to 1 *catty* (17½ ounces) a day towards the end of the punishment. The maximum length of solitary confinement was said to be two months at that time, in the north of China
- special discipline brigades (average length of time 3 months): 1 *catty* a day while undertaking the heaviest work for about 12 hours a day.

More recent accounts indicate that offenders in solitary confinement have their normal food rations reduced by one third.

Offenders undergoing labour-rehabilitation[10] have a slightly better diet than convicted prisoners. In the 850th farm of *Xingkaihu* they are reported to have received, in spring 1958, 90 *catties* of food per person per month, including rice, steamed bread buns, meat and fish, etc. This quantity and quality of food is exceptional, even for labour-rehabilitation offenders, and was granted only because, on this farm, they worked an average of 15 hours a day. For the same reason, food was distributed four or five times a day (whereas usually prisoners have three meals a day). However, their rations were cut dramatically during the Great Leap Forward—from 90 to 50, then 45, 36 and finally 21 *catties* a month. Grain was not available any more and food was served cold. They received a type of feed usually given to pigs, which they tried to supplement by eating leaves, roots and dead birds.

Similar ration cuts affected convicted prisoners at that period. A dramatic reduction of rations occurred also during the "hard years"

(1960-62) when the country was on the verge of famine. Although the food shortage was general, prisoners were among those who suffered most from the famine as they had little chance of supplementing their regular diet. A certain decrease in quantity and quality of food was reported also during the Cultural Revolution (1966-68), but was apparently far less significant than that of 1960-62.

Typical rations seem to have remained at about 40 *catties* a month in the early 1970s. In a labour-reform farm in Gaorong county (Guangdong province), the ration in 1968-71 was 39 *catties* of rice per month per person. In the *Lianping* camp (Guangdong), in 1971-74 a prisoner working about eight hours a day in the fields received the following rations:

- 35 *catties* of rice per month
- 100 to 150 grammes of oil per month
- vegetables (the amount depending on what the prisoners grew)
- meat (depending on the number of pigs raised by the prisoners: when production was good, they could have about 150 grammes of meat once a week.)

On these rations, the prisoners who did not receive extra food from their families were undernourished. The camp regulations prohibited the exchange of food (or other items) between prisoners. Those who received sufficient food from relatives sometimes threw their prison rations into the pig swill and "poor" prisoners tried to steal it at night. If they were caught, a "struggle" meeting was organized against them. In this camp, stealing food is said to have been the most common reason for being "struggled against".

The rations at the *Baoanzhao* farm from the late 1960s to the early 1970s were between 40 and 45 catties of carbohydrate per person per month. The basic diet has been described as follows:

- the main food was maize, millet (between 10 and 20 per cent of the total ration) and red *kaoliang* (a type of sorghum normally given to horses). Rice was given to prisoners only during the four annual festivals (New Year, Spring Festival, 1 May and 1 October)
- 60 grammes of oil a month
- about one teacupful of vegetables at each of the three daily meals
- 50 to 100 grammes of meat only four times a year at the annual festivals

The ration norms were not, according to report, adhered to, as cereals were served in a watery preparation, including the grain husk and skin. Slogans advocating frugality were posted in the farm and those working in the kitchen saved food voluntarily to show their activism. The oil ration, 60 grammes a month, was particularly inadequate for a region with an extremely cold climate.

In 1972, the food rations per person in the *Sangyip* prison of Lhasa (Autonomous Region of Tibet) are reported to have been:

- 1 *catty* of *tsampa* (made from barley) per day (that is, about 30 *catties* per month) and black tea
- half a *catty* (250 grammes) of butter or oil per month (owing to climatic conditions, Tibetans traditionally use large amounts of butter mixed with tea)
- meat once a month
- vegetables (amount depending on what the prisoners grew in the prison garden during their off-duty hours)

Whereas convicted prisoners working in labour-reform farms, camps and prison-factories are given three meals a day, offenders not yet convicted and held for investigation in detention centers are fed only twice a day. They generally either do not work or else do only light work inside the centers. Nevertheless, the obsession with food is the same as in labour camps and is made acute by continuous confinement in the cells.

Rations for detention centers are reported to have been fixed in 1957 at 28 *catties* per person per month. This norm seems to have been slightly reduced later, judging by the accounts of two ex-detainees. Diet in *Hemulang* detention center (west of Canton) from the end of 1966 to the end of 1968 consisted of:

- 25 *catties* of rice a month
- 100 grammes of oil a month
- vegetables at each meal
- no meat at all in the period 1966-67. Towards the end of 1968 cooked dishes, including some meat, were served to detainees every 10 days or so.

Diet in the detention center of *Huiyang* county (Guangdong province) in 1970-72:

- 25 or 26 *catties* of rice a month
- 150 grammes of oil a month
- vegetables (amount depending on what the detainees grew). Four different kinds were served, but they were badly cooked, being boiled until they turned black
- 100-150 grammes of meat only four times a year during the annual festivals. As the meat was fat, and a rare dish for the prisoners, it caused diarrhoea.

These rations were particularly inadequate for detainees coming from the countryside who were used to eating more rice. The detainees who were allowed to go out of the cells to work reportedly tried to steal some of the pigs' food for the hungriest inmates. Those who worked received a supplement of about 50 grammes of rice at each meal (equivalent to an extra 6 *catties* a month). Vegetables were brought to each cell in a dish at mealtimes, but the rice was brought in individual bowls. It was distributed in these before steaming to ensure that everyone had the same amount. However, because the rice was stored in big buckets which were wetter at the bottom than the top, this system did not prevent slight inequalities. When food was brought to the cells, the detainees immediately noticed which bowls were the fullest, and this regularly provoked quarrels.

From one account[11] of conditions in an unidentified detention center during the Cultural Revolution (1967) the rationing norm there was more or less the same as in the places mentioned above. The author of this account, who was detained for 50 days during the spring of 1967, states that each detainee should theoretically receive 400 grammes of rice a day (the equivalent of 24 or 25 *catties* per month); however, he claims that, at that period, detainees in this detention center received only one small bun made of sweet potatoes and two bowls of watery congee (a runny cereal gruel) with a bit of pickle at each meal; that the food did not include any oil and that detainees were constantly hungry.

More recently, wall posters in Peking have alleged that people arrested after the April 1976 demonstrations on Peking's Tian An Men Square were detained in harsh conditions. Many of them were not released until January 1977. According to an account in the French periodical *L'Express*,[12] some of the arrested demonstrators alleged after their release that they had been undernourished in detention and furthermore had had to pay for the food when they were released. The account states that one of them had to pay 11 *yuan*[13] for three months in detention (during which he received only two rolls of maize bread a day), and left prison on a stretcher, unable to stand because he had lost more than 20 kilogrammes in weight. Another recent article published in Hong Kong[14] has also alleged that people detained temporarily in police stations or "reception centers" (transit detention centers)[15] have to pay for their food and keep while in detention.

Although the two accounts above reflect unusually harsh detention conditions which apparently do not normally prevail in detention centers, it is evident that the typical food rations for inmates of detention centers fall far short of their needs. As far as Amnesty International knows, offenders not yet convicted in detention centers cannot improve their regular diet by buying extra food and may be forbidden to receive food parcels from their families until their cases are "decided".

Convicted prisoners held in labour-reform farms, camps and prison-factories may receive parcels of food, clothing and "articles of daily use" (usually toilet articles). The Law on Reform Through Labour does not specify how much extra food is permitted nor how often prisoners may receive parcels. This decision is, in fact, left entirely to the penal institution officials and the right to receive parcels may be denied at any time if a prisoner's behaviour is not judged satisfactory.

The same applies to prisoners' "shopping" rights. There are shopping facilities in some large labour-reform farms and prisons, but none apparently in many others. When these facilities do exist, prisoners who have money may buy some extra food and small items (soap, toothpaste, paper, pen, cigarettes), but the food for sale appears to be available irregularly and to consist of only small amounts of sweets, biscuits, salt and fruit. Basic food (bread, meat, etc.) is never on sale in the "shopping stations".

The *Lianping* camp (Guangdong province) had no "shopping station" in 1974, but some prisoners were appointed once or twice a month to go shopping outside the camp for their fellow inmates. Each prisoner could order only a limited quantity of food (mainly biscuits and sweets), the amount being fixed according to the "mood" of the "discipline and education" warder (*guanjiao*). One prisoner could spend each time, on average, between a few cents and one *yuan* on food and other items. During the annual festivals, they were allowed to spend up to two or three *yuan*.

Even these limited privileges are not available to many prisoners. Those who are known for bad behaviour, as well as those who do not receive extra food or money from their families, have to live on insufficient rations. Through the lack of calories and vitamins, their health may decline quickly if they do not find "illegal" ways of compensating for this deficiency. Prisoners are forbidden to exchange food: apart from small personal articles, they may not keep any extra food, money or other belongings received from their families. For instance, money sent by relatives as well as the one *yuan* pocket-money that, on average, each prisoner receives per month is kept by the authorities and the amount recorded in an account book. On the appointed day, prisoners write a list of what they want to buy, one person is assigned to do the shopping and the sum spent is recorded in an account book. Parcels of food or other items are generally kept in a locked store and prisoners may take out only small amounts at a time. The aim of this system is to prevent not only stealing but also exchanges between prisoners and to allow the authorities to keep a tight control over the prisoners' daily life. These prohibitions and other features of the penal system are in line with the policy that prisoners must "rely on the government" and not on each other for everything.

Labour-rehabilitation offenders receive wages in accordance with their output, from which are deducted the cost of their food and other expenses. After these deductions they are given some pocket-money and the rest of their wages is either sent to their families or kept as a reserve fund for when they are released. Although in the eyes of the law they are citizens and not prisoners, their wages are said to be lower than those they would receive outside the camps.[16]

In general, the treatment of labour-reform and labour-rehabilitation offenders is not substantially different. Although the latter receive slightly better food and have some additional privileges, their work conditions and the discipline to which they are subjected are similar to those of convicted prisoners. The third aspect of conditions in labour-reform institutions examined below concerns convicted and non-convicted offenders equally.

Medical care

According to the law, the reform through labour institutions must, depending on their size, have hospitals, dispensaries or other medical facilities with the necessary equipment.[17]

The medical facilities at the headquarters of some prison complexes or large labour-reform farms have been described to Amnesty International as adequate. There is generally a well-equipped hospital catering for tens of thousands of prisoners from various camps or prisons in a particular area. However, the medical units in the local branches of these large complexes are often deficient and some small camps appear not to be provided with any medical facilities at all. This deficiency is sometimes made more acute by the shortage of medicines and well-trained medical personnel. In line with the policy of making full use of offenders' professional skills, the lack of civilian medical personnel is compensated for by the assignment of prisoner-doctors to hospitals and dispensaries, and to the brigades and companies of large labour-reform farms. At the basic level, however, the prisoners working as doctors are not all qualified practitioners and some have acquired only *ad hoc* and sketchy notions of medicine.

It must be emphasized that, to a certain extent, the lack of proper medical facilities is not limited to penal institutions and thus should not be thought of as deliberate policy. The same could not be said, however, of the prevalent official attitude in camps and prisons towards the inmates' needs, including their need for medical treatment.

Prisoners have often complained that proper medical care is not given to them until they are seriously ill, and some cases have been reported of prisoners who have died of illnesses which were not treated in time. Although responsibility in such cases usually lies with local officials, there is no doubt that their attitude stems from official policy *vis-à-vis* offenders. Self-sacrifice is constantly demanded of prisoners as a proof of reform, and so they are expected to work to the limit of their strength. Often they are not considered worthy of being treated as citizens, and adequate medical attention is granted as a privilege rather than a right.

The medical facilities of the *Baoanzhao* farm (Heilongjiang) have been described to Amnesty International. There is a large hospital capable of accommodating 100 to 200 patients at the farm's head-quarters but it is said to be used mainly to treat cadres and civilians living in the area. If they have permission, prisoners can go to the hospital when they need special medicines or for surgery. Each of the four branch-farms has a dispensary with several dozen beds (there are some 10,000 people at each branch-farm). Prisoners with serious illnesses are sent to this dispensary.

Each brigade (*dadui*) or unit (*danwei*) has a clinic, used for con-sultations, where some medicines are available, but with no special accommodation for sick prisoners. The clinic is staffed with one cadre-doctor (an official of the camp) and two prisoner-doctors, one in charge of surgery and the other of general practice. Some of the prisoners working as doctors in the units are not qualified practitioners but have acquired some medical knowledge while in detention.

Sick prisoners have the right to consult a doctor at the clinic in the evening. If they have a fever, the doctor may write a note recom-mending sick leave. The prisoner must then present the note to the group leader, who takes it to the middle-brigade chief to request permission for the sick leave. The middle-brigade chief, as has been seen, is a cadre from the camp administration, whose permission for sick leave is reported generally to depend on the prisoner's perform-ance and on whether or not it is a period of intensive production. In other words, the decision is not based primarily on the prisoner's state of health.

Prisoners granted sick leave may stay in their cells and rest on the *kang* (brick beds heated underneath, which are common in the north of China). During the day, the doctors visit the patients in their cells. In the late 1960s and early 1970s, the most common diseases on the farm were influenza and fevers. There were limited amounts of medicine—mainly aspirin, penicillin and medicines for skin diseases. During the Great Leap Forward and the "hard" years (1958-59, 1960-62), prisoners received low rations of substitute food and suffered from stomach troubles, ulcers and other symptoms of malnutrition. Many are reported to have died during that period—apparently the only time when large numbers of prisoners showed open discontent and resistance to the authorities.

One camp under the jurisdiction of Peking, situated at Yanjing, [18] is reported to have opened, in 1964, a section for sick and convalescent prisoners transferred from the *Liangxiang* camp [19] together with the medical personnel of a hospital until then established at *Liangxiang*. The only other section at Yanjing consisted of "labour-rehabilitation" offenders working in a steel mill. The sick and convalescent prisoners were judged unfit for "heavy" labour, but were set to work cultivating food crops. Their living conditions were said to be harsh, as the soil was infertile and the climate inclement.

By contrast, prisoners in Peking Prison No. 1 received adequate medical treatment. The prison had a well-equipped, well-staffed hospital big enough for 150 beds, separate surgical and tuberculosis wards and X-ray and dentistry equipment. It has been reported that prisoners in some camps under the jurisdiction of Peking received proper medical treatment after 1962 as a result of steps taken to see that they did, on account of the high death rates recorded during the famine years. Prisoners were then given X-rays and medical examinations twice a year. It is likely that similar measures were taken in other camps, as the whole country had been affected by the famine.

Amnesty International does not know whether this is still the prevailing situation. However, more recent reports continue to mention the inadequacy of medical care. In Guangdong province, the *Lianping* camp, which was opened in 1971 and held more than 2,000 prisoners in 1974, had no medical establishment and no doctor among the official staff of the camp throughout that period. One of the prisoners was a doctor and was probably able to examine prisoners occasionally. However, it is said that sick prisoners were not treated until they became very seriously ill, in which case the doctor from a nearby people's commune was sometimes called in to examine them, and if they were in a desperate state, they were sent to a hospital in the district. Prisoners in this camp lived in primitive conditions when they started building it (in 1971—construction was completed in 1973). In the event of death, the family of the deceased was asked to come to verify that the prisoner had died of natural causes, after which burial could take place.

Officials of the Shanghai Teachers' Training College spoke of a noteworthy case to a foreign journalist, Ian Mackenzie, in September 1977. They were giving examples of the persecution suffered by several veteran cadres of the college under the influence of the "gang of four" after the Cultural Revolution. Among the victims was a senior cadre from the college who, despite poor health, was sent for reform through labour in Heilongjiang province. "He returned to Shanghai a very sick man and died shortly afterwards."[20]

Discipline and treatment

Strict control is maintained at all times over the prisoners, not only as a security measure but also as a means of making their daily life and behaviour the subject of public debate.

Disciplinary measures are provided for by the law for "troublesome" prisoners, and each detention center, labour camp and prison has internal regulations which are usually read to the prisoners upon arrival and posted permanently in the cells. These regulations vary slightly from one institution to another. They usually include injunctions to reform as well as disciplinary instructions.

In detention centers,[21] detainees are most commonly told:

- to study Chairman Mao's works diligently and reform their thoughts
- not to exchange information on their case with other people
- not to share (food) or exchange objects
- not to form "cliques" inside the cell
- not to yell, fight or smoke
- not to spread rumours and counter-revolutionary propaganda
- to denounce other people's mistakes, breaches of regulations and criminal activities.

As can be seen, these regulations aim mainly at preventing detainees from establishing relationships with one another and encourage them to report on each other.

The rules in prisons and labour camps are more or less the same, but place more emphasis on discipline and work. They also include moral injunctions to reform and to watch each other, such as:

- in all circumstances obey orders and listen to instructions
- labour actively: if you gain "merits" making up for your crimes you will become a "new man" early
- study actively and diligently; reform your thoughts

- denounce and wage an open struggle against bad elements and criminal activities
- remember the great policy: "confession [frankness] deserves leniency, resistance deserves severity".

Any slackness of discipline, even over the minor details of daily routine, has to be accounted for by the prisoners themselves. If a prisoner who has committed a "mistake" does not take the initiative in making a self-criticism, fellow members of the group will denounce and criticize him or her. Failure to report on another prisoner is taken as implicit approval of the culprit's behaviour and hence means running the risk of being criticized oneself.

The general attitude of each prisoner—at work, during the "study" period or vis-à-vis fellow inmates—is carefully recorded during periodic examinations of everyone's "performance", when some are singled out for reward or punishment. The law lists the following behaviour punishable directly by the camp or prison administration:

1. hindering the reform of other offenders
2. lack of care for or damage to production implements (tools and machines)
3. laziness or deliberately slow work
4. other breaches of the rules of administration.[22]

As can be seen, the law does not give a comprehensive list of the situations in which punishment can be inflicted. It is equally imprecise about the actual punishments which could be meted out: "warning, demerit, solitary confinement or other punishment".[23]

Other articles of the Law on Reform Through Labour are slightly more specific about some punishments, although not about the circumstances calling for them: in prisons, solitary confinement may be used "in case of necessity" (Article 14); instruments of restraint may be used in cases of violence or "dangerous actions" by the prisoners (Article 46); visits, correspondence and receipt of parcels may be denied or limited in "special circumstances" (Article 57); in addition, Article 50, which deals with the standards of clothing and food for prisoners, prohibits only "unauthorized" reduction of the norms, which implies that there may be authorized reductions.

In addition to breaches of discipline (or violations of the "rules of administration", to use the official terminology), the law also lists the kinds of behaviour (considered "crimes") for which prisoners can be brought before a court and receive an additional sentence:

1. riot, or commission of, or incitement to, violent acts
2. escape or organization of escapes

3. destruction of construction work or important public property
4. open resistance to labour despite repeated education
5. other acts that seriously break the law.[24]

There is a similarity between what is considered a "criminal" act in point 4 above and what is considered as a simple infraction of discipline in points 2 and 3 listed on p. 119. The difference is only one of degree. As regards the "destruction of construction work" (point 3 above) and the "damage to production equipment" (point 2 of the discipline violations), the law does not make it clear whether intentional destruction is meant, which suggests that prisoners might also be punished for accidental damages caused at work.

On the other hand, the law is slightly more specific about the situations in which a prisoner may be rewarded. They are as follows:

1. regular observance of discipline, diligent study and genuine demonstration of repentance and reform
2. dissuading other offenders from unlawful conduct, or providing information on counter-revolutionary activity inside or outside prisons which is confirmed by investigation
3. active labour, fulfilment or over-fulfilment of production tasks
4. special accomplishments in conserving raw materials and taking care of public property
5. particular diligence or creativity in the study, use or teaching of technical skills
6. contribution to eliminating disasters or major incidents and avoiding loss
7. other acts beneficial to the people and the state.[25]

The rewards in order of importance are to receive a commendation, a material reward, a "merit", a reduction of sentence or conditional release. The two last are granted only after the camp or prison officials' recommendation has been submitted to the Public Security agency in charge of review and approved by the appropriate people's court.

As regards rewards or punishments which do not require this type of approval, camp and prison administrators are allowed considerable latitude in defining what constitutes "good" or "bad" behaviour. Generally the assessment of the prisoners' attitude is made by a political "instructor" (*guanjiao*) assigned to a group of a hundred or several hundred prisoners. The "instructor" is in charge of discipline and political education, and, together with the other cadres supervising a group, makes periodical recommendations for sanctions and rewards which are reviewed by the camp or prison director or his deputies.

One can distinguish between "ordinary" punishments and "formal" ones. The former are those which may be inflicted at any time for minor "misconduct". They include: reduction of food rations for a short period; temporary loss of the right to receive visits, parcels or correspondence; loss of small privileges (pocket-money, shopping); being forbidden temporarily to read newspapers or books or participate in cultural activities; subjection to either criticism meetings, followed by oral or written self-criticism or, in more serious cases, to a "struggle" meeting.

Such punishments are usually inflicted for failure to fulfil production norms or for breaches of discipline in the daily routine. Persistent or repeated "misconduct" is punished more severely. The reasons for punishing a prisoner may be quite arbitrary. A former prisoner, Bao Ruowang (Jean Pasqualini) has described the circumstances in which a prisoner called Xu (Hsu) was not allowed to receive a parcel in 1961 at the *Qinghe* farm.[26]

According to Bao Ruowang, Xu's brother, a young army soldier, had come for an authorized visit on the eve of Chinese New Year and brought food parcels for Xu. A zealous guard immediately remarked that the food weighed more than the permitted 5 kilogrammes. When the young soldier tried to argue, an "education and discipline warder" (instructor) intervened, after being duly briefed by the guard. Not only was Xu's brother lectured about his serious lack of ideological principle for bringing a "counter-revolutionary" "delicacies" that peasants and workers did not enjoy, but the warder noted his unit number and the name of his commanding officer, probably to make a report about the young soldier's behaviour. The warder asked him to take back the parcels, saying of Xu, who was present: "This prisoner isn't entitled to any gifts. And, by the way, he would tell you himself that he doesn't need any parcels from you. He lacks nothing here. Isn't that right?" Xu could only assent obediently.[27]

This type of attitude towards prisoners is not unusual. Submission to the guards and cadres is an absolute requirement and humiliation is often considered necessary for "reform". Routine methods are used to remind them that they are "criminals". For instance, they have to address the guards and officials by their titles instead of calling them "comrade", which is the normal form of address in the PRC. Moreover, prisoners may not themselves be called "comrade" as they are not considered to be citizens.

Prisoners criticized for some misdemeanour have to adopt a humble attitude in order to be "forgiven". This means that they must not only make a thorough self-criticism as regards the misdeed but also acknowledge that they are not "worthy of the Government's care". Any attitude indicating a lack of humility is liable to result in punishment.

"Formal" punishments are usually announced during special meetings held once or twice a year, depending on the place. These meetings are preceded by a period of intense ideological mobilization which, in winter, is sometimes called the *dongxun*, "winter discipline training". The *dongxun* may last several weeks. Each prisoner's attitude during the previous year or six months is examined and some are singled out for criticism. At the end of this period, all prisoners are assembled for an "award/punishment meeting", to hear the result of this special "training".

These periodic "trainings" and "award/punishment meetings" are held mainly to impress on prisoners in a formal way that their reform (and, by implication, release) depends entirely on themselves. Regularly, therefore, a few examples are selected for rewards and punishments. Occasionally a particularly serious case may be singled out for capital punishment. Prisoners have reported that, although rare, executions are sometimes carried out in labour-reform camps as exemplary punishment for serious violations of the law (escaping or attempting to escape, "counter-revolutionary" activities, etc.). [28]

The "formal" punishments announced during "award/punishment meetings" are generally imposed on prisoners who have been noted for bad behaviour during the preceding months—that is, who are likely to have already been given ordinary punishments. The mildest "formal" punishments are "warnings" and "demerits". Both are simple records of bad behaviour, a demerit being more serious than a warning; but an accumulation of several warnings or demerits results in a harsher punishment (see below). The most severe punishments are: solitary confinement, work under special discipline and increase of sentence. Work under special discipline means heavier work than usual, being forbidden to speak to other prisoners, reduced rations and sometimes the wearing of fetters.

A former prisoner (who has asked to remain anonymous) told Amnesty International of his experience of punishments on a labour-reform farm where he was a prisoner from 1958 to 1969 and then kept on as a "free-worker" until 1972. For several consecutive years he was classified as "resistant" to work because of his inadequate output and "bad" attitude at work. Consequently "demerits" were given to him regularly during the annual "award/punishment" meetings. Twice, after receiving two or three consecutive "demerits", he was punished by solitary confinement, each time for more than three months. His persistent "bad" attitude was further punished when his original term of imprisonment was extended for another two years, which he spent on the same farm.

For his unit of more than 500 prisoners there was only one solitary confinement cell, but two or three prisoners could, he said, be confined "in the same room" when necessary. The "solitary confinement" cell was in the prisoners' dormitory and he described the conditions in this way:

"The cell was very small, just about large enough to lie down in. There was only straw on the floor and a small window in one wall. The cell was guarded day and night by 'activists' (zealous or highly-regarded prisoners). The food received in solitary confinement is about one-third less than the normal rations. Once a day a bucket is passed in to the punished prisoner to evacuate the excrement [*sic*]. During the seasonal production [period of intensive work] prisoners in solitary confinement may be allowed to go out to work. They are escorted to the place of work by activists and have to work harder than other prisoners. During work they are forbidden to talk to other prisoners. In any case, other prisoners would run away if a punished prisoner tried to do so. In case of illness, a prisoner in solitary confinement may be treated. The length of the punishment depends on how thoroughly the prisoner recognizes his 'mistakes', guarantees that he will labour actively, reform his thoughts, side actively with the Government and struggle against the 'bad things' and 'bad elements'. The maximum length of solitary confinement would normally be half a year."

The duration of solitary confinement apparently varies from camp to camp, but conditions are generally similar to those described above. In other words, solitary confinement is not only a period of physical isolation, but a punishment involving confinement in a tiny cell and a significant reduction in food rations. In the *Lianping* camp in Guangdong province, prisoners put in solitary confinement from 1971 to 1974 had their normal rations reduced by one-third and were reportedly held in similar conditions to those described above, with two important exceptions: they were taken out of the cell once a week for a bath and they were not allowed to work, but stayed in the tiny cell for the whole of the punishment.[29]

Conditions in solitary confinement generally prompt prisoners to recognize "their guilt" very quickly when an "instructor" (discipline warder) checks on their state of mind after one or two weeks. However, in the *Lianping* camp, offenders found guilty or suspected of planning to escape are said to have been kept in solitary confinement for several months.

According to a Tibetan refugee, conditions in solitary confinement for a group of Tibetans held for interrogation in Shekar (south-west of Lhasa) in 1959 were particularly harsh.[30] In order to extract a confession from them, some detainees were allegedly put in leg-irons in tiny cells resembling "coffin-like wooden cupboards", not large enough to stand, sit or sleep in properly. Food was passed in to them through a small hatch in the door and a tin, emptied once a week, served as a toilet inside the cell. The detainees, according to the refugee, soon confessed under these conditions.

The same Tibetan refugee also said that a "resistant" prisoner named Shikya Chanzo Nangnam was put in solitary confinement in 1960 in *Karkang* prison (in Shigatse, west of Lhasa) and was still there four years later because, throughout the period, he refused to recant. The refugee described Shikya Chanzo Nangnam as a "bearded" monk from the Panchen Lama's Tashilumpo monastery.

Officials in penal institutions occasionally use handcuffs and fetters to break the resistance of an offender. This method is said to be used both in labour-reform institutions and in detention centers.

The Law for Reform Through Labour specifies that instruments of restraint may be used only where there is a possibility of escape, violence or "other dangerous acts" on the part of offenders, and that they must be removed immediately when these circumstances are eliminated".[31] However, there is evidence that the law has been interpreted in a broad way by local officials. A political offender mentioned earlier (Chapter II, p. 44) was reported to have been chained for 24 hours for shouting "counter-revolutionary" slogans and the chains attached in such a way as to leave him in a painful position.

Prisoners' accounts of the use of handcuffs or fetters clearly reveal an infringement of the law, since the devices are used as a punishment and not to prevent prisoners from being violent or escaping. In his account of his life in prison, Duan Kewen, a former Guomindang official imprisoned from 1951 to 1975, alleges that he wore heavy fetters for about five years, from 1951 to 1956.[32] He also alleges that in Changchun Labour-Reform Brigade No. 1, where he was held during 1953 and 1954, over one-third of the prisoners in his middle-brigade (which consisted of more than 500 prisoners) wore fetters, even at work.[33]

According to another report received by Amnesty International, major offenders held in the *Yingde* camp (Guangdong province) in 1967 also wore fetters. Unlike the prisoners spoken of by Duan Kewen, they did not work.

In the case of convicted offenders in prison-factories, labour-reform farms or camps, handcuffs or fetters appear to be used mainly as supplementary punishments: prisoners put in solitary confinement or to work under special discipline are sometimes chained during part or all of the period of punishment.

Non-convicted detainees in detention centers have been handcuffed or fettered either as a disciplinary measure (for a breach of regulations) or to hasten confession.

Bao Ruowang has described how a detainee, newly arrived at Peking's Grass Mist Lane Detention Center in 1958, was led in chains to solitary confinement after being subjected to a "struggle" session in his cell:

> ". . . he could barely move. His feet were in fetters, an iron bar a foot long, ringed at both ends to pass around the ankles. Bolts held the rings fast; two chains rose from the middle of the bar to the wrists, which themselves were joined by another chain. In all, the outfit weighed thirty-two pounds. The prisoner was obliged to carry the vertical chain from his feet looped several times, since it was long enough to drag on the floor and that was forbidden."[34]

According to Bao Ruowang, this case was not exceptional and, although the restraining devices were not always as heavy and complicated as those described above, many detainees wore handcuffs and shackles for varying periods during the two years that, on average, they spent in detention before being sentenced.

One account published in Hong Kong[35] makes reference to the extensive use of handcuffs and chains in a detention center at the height of the Cultural Revolution (1967). The author states that he was arrested in February 1967 and held for more than 50 days in the detention center (which he does not identify). He describes the harsh conditions of detention and reports that all newly arrived prisoners were handcuffed, some with their hands in front, some behind, for 3 to 10 days or for longer if they were considered uncooperative by their interrogators. The handcuffs were apparently very tight, permitting hardly any movement of the hands. Detainees wearing them suffered discomfort and pain, and could eat and urinate only in humiliating positions. According to this report, some "courageous" detainees who protested against their arrest and treatment were punished. An actor from the local opera company who did so was put in fetters weighing 18 pounds, which practically prevented him from walking. A young worker went on hunger strike in protest against his arbitrary arrest and treatment but stopped his strike after being summoned by his interrogators: the author of this report did not know what made him change his mind but says that as soon as the young worker started eating again, he was tied behind with the heaviest and most painful manacles that the author had seen in this detention center.

According to this report, arrests and releases followed the ups and downs of the local power struggle during the Cultural Revolution. After one change of power in the area in July 1967, the Public Security Bureau Chief and the Director of this detention center, who had been responsible for the malpractices mentioned, were harshly denounced in public for having "cruelly suppressed the revolutionary masses" during the preceding months.

It must be emphasized that the above account refers to a period of widespread violence and that such a systematic use of handcuffs and shackles does not appear to have been a common practice before the Cultural Revolution. Many ex-prisoners, however, have reported that instruments of restraint are used occasionally by interrogators to break the resistance of detainees during investigation, and the practice is said to continue.

The suffering caused by such practices, even if their use is "limited", is apparently not regarded by officials who employ them as a contravention of Article 5 of the Law on Reform Through Labour, which strictly prohibits cruel treatment and corporal punishment (torture).

Amnesty International has too little information to be sure what the current prevailing practice is over the use of instruments of restraint such as shackles and fetters; as far as is known, the legal provisions authorizing their use in specific circumstances—worded in such a way as to allow a broad interpretation—are still in force.

Throughout the country over the past 10 years, many people detained for investigation seem to have been subjected to other forms of harassment. Both wall posters put up in the streets by individuals and, more recently, the official press itself have revealed numerous cases of maltreatment. Some examples are given below.

According to the Agence France Presse (AFP) correspondent in Peking, a wall poster signed Chung Chun-te appeared in the capital on 25 June 1974, denouncing the conditions in which the author had been held in a Peking detention center a month before. He had been arrested on 26 May for putting up large-character posters and held for four days in this center before being transferred to his home province of Jilin. According to the AFP report, on the evening of his first day in prison, Chung Chun-te protested when a young boy in his cell was refused permission to go out for a drink of tea and subsequently lost consciousness. Chung Chun-te's action was later punished in this way:

> "I objected aloud to that refusal and was punished. On 28 May
> in the morning a violent fight broke out in the prison, I had

nothing to do with it, but a staff member shoved me through a door and I was at once ringed by four people who held my legs, twisted my arms and grabbed my head. They thrashed me before tying me up with ropes.

"My body covered with mud and sweat, I was thrown into room No. 35. I was placed on my stomach with my arms and legs held above my back by ropes, exactly in the position of a boat. The door of the room was double-locked and I had to stay there like that for two hours with the sweat streaming down my face like a river.

"My limbs quickly became numb, and when I was finally untied I was incapable of getting back into a normal position by myself. I had to be helped to make my arms work again. For a long time they refused to obey me."[36]

In the *New York Times Magazine* of 4 December 1977, Harrison E. Salisbury cited the cases of artists and writers detained after the Cultural Revolution, who were rehabilitated after the purge of the "gang of four". He reported that most of these intellectuals had suffered harassment, sometimes even torture, while in detention. Among the examples given by Harrison Salisbury was that of Liu Shih-kun, a pianist and the son-in-law of Marshal Ye Jianying.[37] He was reportedly approached by "representatives of Miss Chiang's clique"[38] to give information on Marshal Ye and Zhou Enlai. "When the pianist refused, his fingers were broken. He was sent to prison for a five-year term and held incommunicado." Harrison Salisbury also cites the case of a composer, Liu Fan, who was confined for two years in his narrow office at the Shanghai Conservatory: he said that he was not permitted to go home to see his wife and family and that he was constantly exposed to violent invective from those surrounding him in a "circle of rage". "He was humiliated, spat upon, beaten, his arms twisted behind his back, his head forced to the floor."[39]

The maltreatment of detainees and arbitrary arrests carried out since the Cultural Revolution are now officially attributed to the influence of the purged leaders.[40] The factional struggles that continued in power groups after the Cultural Revolution did indeed involve numerous arbitrary arrests, and created a climate conducive to brutality and illegal practices. However, some of the forms of harassment described by victims of the "gang of four" were used long before the Cultural Revolution. Intimidation and humiliation have always been part of interrogation techniques and, in spite of official instructions not to extract "forced" confessions, harsher methods have sometimes been used. In 1963, for instance, a document from the CCP Central Committee giving instructions on how to carry out the "Socialist Education Movement" in the country-side stated: "Some places have violated law and discipline by pouncing upon, waging struggle against and torturing people at random."[41] It noted that although these were isolated cases, serious attention should be paid to them, and it prohibited the application of such methods to those "among the masses" who had "short-comings and mistakes". Apparently the same prohibition did not apply to the "very few people who are resolutely antagonistic to the people".

Physical torture is prohibited by law and is generally not inflicted on prisoners. Quite often, however, people brought to "struggle" sessions are subjected to intense psychological pressure, molested and sometimes even beaten up. Bao Ruowang has given the following description of the "struggle" session:

"It is a peculiarly Chinese invention, combining intimidation, humiliation and sheer exhaustion. Briefly described, it is an intellectual gang-beating of one man by many, sometimes even thousands, in which the victim has no defence, even the truth.[42]

". . . There is a system and a rationale behind it all . . . A man must be made to confess before he is punished, even if his punishment has been decided beforehand."[43]

". . . If a denunciation leads to a Struggle, the victim is well advised to submit immediately, because there is never any time limit to a Struggle: it can go on indefinitely if the leaders of the game feel that not enough contrition has developed. Like all the other non-physical interrogation techniques, the purpose is to bring the victim to accept anything that may be judged for him. Thus a Struggle is rarely resolved quickly; that would be too easy. At the beginning, even if the victim tells the truth or grovellingly admits to any accusation hurled at him, his every word will be greeted with insults and shrieks of contradiction. He is ringed by jeering, hating faces, screaming in his ear, spitting; fists swipe menacingly close to him and everything he says is branded a lie. At the end of the day he is led to a room, locked up, given some food and left with the promise that the next day will be even worse.[44]

". . . After three or four days the victim begins inventing sins he has never committed, hoping that an admission monstrous enough might win him a reprieve. After a week of Struggling he is prepared to go to any lengths."[45]

According to recent official Chinese sources, "struggle" sessions are still used against political offenders. From the end of 1976 until 1978, many local officials were brought to mass meetings or rallies for "criticism and struggle" in the course of the campaign against the "gang of four" and their followers. Such rallies were organized throughout the country and the campaign was still going on in early 1978. A few examples follow.

In June 1977, three disgraced officials were subjected to "mass criticism" at a rally in Yunnan province, according to a local radio broadcast. The three were Chu Ko-chia, an alternate member of the CCP Central Committee, Huang Chao-chi, an army officer and an official called Liu Yin-ming. According to a Reuter report from Peking, the radio said that the crowd's hatred erupted like a volcano as the three were "denounced, exposed and criticized" by their former comrades.[46]

A radio broadcast from Lhasa (Autonomous Region of Tibet) announced in September 1977 that a rally had been held in the People's Stadium in Lhasa to "criticize and struggle against that sinister henchman of the gang of four in our region". The rally was held on 4 September and attended by 10,000 people.[47]

In August 1977, Shenyang Radio (Liaoning province) reported that since 20 July many units had held meetings to "wage face-to-face struggles against the henchmen and followers of the gang of four" in the province. According to the broadcast, one of the accused was criticized "face-to-face" "until he had to admit helplessly that he had long colluded with that sworn follower of the gang of four . . . He had to admit the numerous crimes that they had committed to oppose the Party and the Center."[48]

The New China News Agency reported in July 1978 that two former officials from Sichuan province, Liu Jieting and his wife Zhang Xiting, were brought to 53 "criticism and struggle rallies" in the province between August 1977 and February 1978. The Agency stated that their arrest had been decided by the CCP Central Committee. They were accused of having persecuted cadres and organized "large-scale struggle" in Sichuan during the Cultural Revolution, as well as of collusion with the "gang of four".[49] A Reuter report from Peking on 19 October 1977 indicated that the two main targets of the struggle in the province (probably Liu and his wife) had been held for investigation in Peking before being sent back to Sichuan to be "screened in isolation" and "put to the struggle".

The stress created by "struggle" meetings has in some cases been so great that the victims have tried to commit suicide—many people are said to have killed themselves during the successive purification campaigns since 1949.[50] The present campaign against the "gang of four" is apparently no exception. Unconfirmed reports have mentioned recent cases of suicide. In the spring of 1977 wall posters at the Fudan University of Shanghai reported that Ho Shih-hsun, the Vice-President of the University Party Committee, committed suicide by jumping from a window at the University after being subjected to "mass criticism" for being an alleged supported of the "gang of four".[51]

Notes

1 The *tongjiyuan*, literally "statistician", is not necessarily a technician, but an "activist" who has to see to the details of work allocation and labour norms.

2 The main provisions of this law were examined in Chapter III, pp. 75-80.

3 See Cohen, op. cit., p. 260; White, op. cit., p. 196.

4 Until recently intellectuals were identified in China as the "ninth notorious category", coming at the end of a list of the "bad classes and elements". The Chinese official press revealed in 1977 many instances of intellectuals being discriminated against, harassed or imprisoned in previous years.

5 Act for Reform Through Labour, Article 50.

6 See Hu Yu-pai's report in White, op. cit., p. 200. This process of evaluation has been confirmed by other reports.

7 1 *catty* (*jin*) = ½ kilogramme.

8 Rationing of food in proportion to work performance was reportedly first tried out in 1955 in one of the earliest labour camps in the Peking area, the "New Life Brick Kiln", east of Peking in Tongzhou district, which was later gradually turned over to civilians. The maximum ration (Grade A) was fixed at 64 *catties* but, according to report, only 55 *catties* were given to the most outstanding workers. In order to receive a Grade A ration, a prisoner had to carry 2,500 bricks per work shift or to make 60 trips pushing a one-wheeled cart filled each time with 100 bricks. See Bao Ruowang, op. cit., for details about rationing norms in the 1960s.

9 Or 200 grammes.

10 See Chapter III, p. 80.

11 "The lowest strata prison" (*zui diceng jianyu*) by Chen Lin, in a Chinese-language Hong Kong review, *Nanbeiji* of 16 December 1976.

12 Jacques and Claudie Broyelle, "Comment vivent les Chinois", *L'Express*, 23-29 January 1978.

13 One *yuan* is equivalent to slightly more than half of one US dollar.

14 "The Supervision and Control System of Mainland China after the Cultural Revolution" by Wen Sang, in *Huang He*, No. 3, 25 April 1977.

15 In Guangdong province a number of police stations and reception centers are reported to have been controlled, from the Cultural Revolution until recently, either by the "Workers Inspectors Brigade" (a civilian police organization) or by the military authorities, and not by the Public Security agencies.

16 According to White, op. cit., p. 200, offenders in a large labour-rehabilitation farm in southern Guangdong province received wages ranging from 16 *yuan* to 30 *yuan* a month in 1958-61.

17 Act for Reform Through Labour, Article 53.

18 Yanjing is some 95 km. north-west of Peking.

19 The *Liangxiang* camp, located south of Peking, was Peking's "Eighth Labour Reform Brigade". (See Bao Ruowang, op. cit., pp. 265-266.)

20 Mackenzie, op. cit.

21 See also the rules of Peking's Grass Mist Lane Detention Center given in Bao Ruowang, op. cit., p. 47.

22 Act for Reform Through Labour, Article 69.

23 ibid.

24 ibid., Article 71.

25 ibid., Article 68.

26 Bao Ruowang, op. cit., pp. 225-228.

27 ibid.

28 One case is cited by Duan Kewen, in "The Narration of a War Criminal", *Shijie Ribao* (World Journal) of 25 October 1976. See also Bao Ruowang, op. cit., p. 187. It has also been reported to Amnesty International that between 1971 and 1974, one official announcement was made in the *Lianping* camp (Guangdong province) that three prisoners had been executed in a nearby camp for attempting to escape.

29 See also Bao Ruowang, op. cit., pp. 126-132—his account of his experience of solitary confinement in a "transit center" in Peking.

30 See Appendix 3, pp. 155-157, for more details on these cases.

31 Act for Reform Through Labour, Article 46.

32 Duan Kewen, op. cit., Part I, 2 November 1976. Duan, a former Major-General of the Guomindang, was arrested in the early 1950s and released by special amnesty in 1975 with other high-ranking Guomindang officials. He was among those who left the PRC with official permission after their release.

33 ibid., 19 October 1976.

34 Bao Ruowang, op. cit., p. 59.

35 "The lowest strata prison" (*zui diceng jianyu*) by Chen Lin, *Nanbeiji* No. 79, December 1976.

36 René Flipo, AFP, Peking, 25 June 1974.

37 Marshal Ye Jiangying (Yeh Chien-ying), Minister of National Defence, was re-elected Vice-Chairman of the CCP Central Committee at the XI Congress of the CCP in August 1977.

38 "Miss Chiang" is Jiang Qing (Chiang Ching, Mao's widow) who was arrested as one of the "gang of four" in October 1976.

39 "Now it's China's Cultural thaw" by Harrison E. Salisbury, in *New York Times Magazine* of 4 December 1977.

40 Before the purge of the "gang of four" in 1976, former Vice-Chairman Lin Biao and important regional leaders who disappeared in 1971 after an alleged attempted *coup* were held responsible for the wave of repression which immediately followed the Cultural Revolution in 1968-71.

41 "Provisions of Certain Concrete Policies of the CCP Central Committee concerning the Socialist Education Movement in the Rural Areas (Draft) September 1963", in *Documents of the Chinese Communist Party Central Committee, September 1956-April 1969*, Vol. I, Union Research Institute, Hong Kong, 1971, p. 765.

42 Bao Ruowang, op. cit., p. 58.

43 ibid., p. 59.

44 ibid., p. 60.

45 ibid., p. 61.

46 David Rogers, Reuter, Peking, 29 June 1977.

47 SWB, FE/5614, of 14 September 1977.

48 Radio broadcast from Shenyang on 8 August 1977, in SWB, FE/5590 of 16 August 1977.

49 New China News Agency, 14 July 1978; see SWB, FE/5867 of 18 July 1978.

50 See Chapter I, p. 17. Suicides were particularly frequent during the Cultural Revolution. See Harrison Salisbury, op. cit.

51 Report by Yvonne Preston from Peking, in the Australian paper *National Times*, 13-18 June 1977.

Reform, Releases and Amnesties

China's penal policy, as defined in law and official documents, is based on the principle that offenders should be "reformed"—both in order to prevent them from committing further crimes after release and so that they may be "transformed into new men" through a thorough reform program involving a change of outlook and progressive adjustment to new standards of behaviour.

In addition to compulsory labour, therefore, offenders are subjected to compulsory "political education". The Chinese penal system does not simply make such education compulsory: it also requires that all prisoners demonstrate that they "voluntarily" accept their reform; that they recognize that their past behaviour was "criminal" and that they participate actively in their own program of reform.

The Law on Reform Through Labour states that the purpose of such reform is to "expose the essence of crime", "to eliminate criminal thoughts", "to establish new concepts of morality", "*to educate offenders about admitting their guilt*[1] and observing the law, about current political events, about labour and production, and about culture".[2]

The reform program, therefore, includes both political education and ideological or "thought" reform.

Offenders not yet convicted held in detention centers also have to undergo a program of reform.

The law gives general instructions on the way to carry out such reform and specifies that the offenders' observance of discipline and behaviour at work and study shall be recorded "at any time".[3] Individual dossiers are therefore compiled to record the details of each prisoner's life and behaviour.

Although the general methods for achieving ideological reform are specified by the law and are quite similar in all penal institutions, the day-to-day supervision of prisoners' reform is left to the prison and camp officials. Local officials have wide powers to decide on what is the best way of encouraging individual prisoners to reform themselves. Their judgements, obviously, may be subjective and therefore in danger of being arbitrary. Moreover, as indicated in Chapter IV, the incentives to reform are not based only on positive encouragements but include a system of punishments.

In spite of official requirements that offenders should "voluntarily" acknowledge their need for reform, they are, in fact, left with no free choice. As nonconformity with the rigid standards of behaviour imposed by official policy may lead to severe punishment and ultimately to an increase of sentence, the majority of offenders generally feels obliged to comply with them.

Another aspect of the penal policy examined below concerns the forceful "retention" or placement of offenders at the end of their sentences. The information in this chapter is based mainly on former prisoners' accounts and on official legal documents.[4]

Political education

Political education (*zhengzhi jiaoyu*) is carried out during the daily "study sessions". An "ordinary" study session consists of assigned reading and discussion of newspaper articles or documents of particular importance. In the evening prisoners are assembled according to their cells or groups (*xiaozu*) for one or two hours. The group comprises on average 10 to 15 prisoners. The group leader directs the "study" and the deputy leader or a prisoner is appointed to take notes. The group leaders have generally been instructed in advance by the "discipline and education" warder on the subjects to raise.

After explaining a text, the group leader asks each prisoner in turn to comment on it. This process is generally a mere formality: most prisoners limit themselves to approving whatever is the official line, possibly making some comparison with their previous way of thinking on the subject, acknowledging, if necessary, that this was wrong and that they are trying to correct their thoughts.

When newspapers are available to prisoners, they are generally the *People's Daily* and/or a local newspaper which also presents official views. In some labour-reform farms and prisons, a "labour-reform paper" (*laogai bao*) which is not available to the public is circulated among the prisoners every week. It is apparently published by the province's Public Security Department and summarizes the achievements of various labour-reform units, as well as giving some national and international news. In some penal institutions, prisoners also have access to a few selected books, generally authorized works on political theory or technical matters. Prisoners whose behaviour is not considered satisfactory may be prohibited from reading, and information may be withheld by the authorities in special circumstances. This was apparently the case in the detention center of Huiyang county (Guangdong province) after the fall of Lin Biao in

1971. According to a former detainee who was held in this center from 1970 to 1972, all publications containing Lin Biao's photograph were suddenly confiscated in October 1971, newspapers were not available and new arrivals were instructed by the detention center authorities not to tell other inmates what was happening in the country.

Even when newspapers are available, acquiring information is not the aim of the "study" and prisoners may read only during their free time. The "study" is an educational exercise to make prisoners express and correct their thoughts about current political events. The texts selected are usually extracts from editorials or theoretical articles of political significance, or else summaries of official reports on party congresses or national conferences, on a change in external policy or a new economic or political campaign. They can also be publications intended to encourage prisoners to confess their guilt. For instance, non-convicted offenders held in the Huiyang detention center mentioned above were once given a text to study which related how a Guomindang commander surrendered to communist troops during the civil war. From this example of surrender, the detainees were encouraged to "open their heart" (*jiaoxin*) to the "Government"– that is, to confess and reveal all their thoughts to the warders. Similar "stimulation" to confession, as well as other forms of pressure, may also be used to make convicted prisoners confess their "misdeeds", especially when a "confession" campaign is launched.[5]

Although the study is a formality in the sense that the correct answers are always predetermined by official policy, it is not a shallow process. On the contrary, it is the starting point of a profound examination of each prisoner's way of thinking. The notes taken during the "study" are forwarded at the end of the session to the "instructor" (discipline and education warder) who supervises several groups of prisoners. The instructor may point out a lack of understanding or "improper" thoughts on the part of some prisoners. At the next study session or at the end of the week, the prisoners are asked to review their standpoint. Group leaders may also, of their own accord, ask prisoners to "reflect" (*fansheng*) on their mistaken ideas.

The group leaders are generally prisoners who are well thought of and trusted by the authorities. They are usually selected from among offenders having a good class and political background who have received relatively short sentences—sometimes former cadres or Party members who have an above-average level of political understanding.[6]

Thought-reform

The official term for "thought-reform" is *sixiang gaizao*, which can also be translated as "ideological reform". Thought-reform starts with routine weekly "self-examination" sessions, as well as with "criticism" or "struggle" meetings to which an individual prisoner may be subjected at any time for misconduct.

The daily study session is not always devoted to the reading and discussion of printed material. Frequently the group leader will start the session by reviewing the day's problems and asking some prisoners to account for their behaviour and others to criticize them. The group leader may also give a "sincere talk" (*tanxin*, literally "talk heart") to individual prisoners to make them realize their mistakes, and they then have to make a thorough self-criticism. Prisoners who defend their position are criticized more and more harshly by fellow inmates until they recognize that they were "thinking along the wrong lines", or they may be punished immediately.

A former prisoner, who had been held in 1968 in the prison at Sechen Ho (*Shiquanhe*, Autonomous Region of Tibet), reported that during the five months he was there, seven prisoners were punished by solitary confinement, either because they had complained about their treatment or because they did not express "proper thoughts" during the political education sessions. He also said that all of them were kept in solitary confinement for at least the five months that he himself spent in prison. The daily study sessions were held from 8.30 p.m. to 9.00 p.m. by groups (*xiaozu*) of about 12 prisoners. Prisoners had to submit their views on the subject in hand to the two officials conducting the sessions. Those who refused to do so, under the pretext of ignorance, were, according to this report, branded "enemies of socialism" and threatened with solitary confinement.

Similarly, prisoners who are criticized by other inmates in their group cannot for long resist the pressure without being punished. Neither can the group avoid denouncing prisoners who make themselves conspicuous by unorthodox thoughts or commit some misdeed. Mutual denunciations are, like self-criticism, compulsory. Prisoners are asked to "rely on the government" and to prove that they are doing so. In practice this means reporting all their thoughts, including what they know about other prisoners. Mutual reporting is such an intrinsic part of the system that prisoners may report not only the misconduct of other inmates but also mere suspicions about them.

One study session every week is usually devoted to a general "self-examination" (*jiantao*). The session might start with a theme prompted by the current national ideological trend, such as "criticism of revisionism", but more often it is a simple review of prisoners' behaviour during the past week. In both cases, the process is similar.

Each prisoner has to give an account of his or her behaviour during the preceding few days and to analyse any misdeeds. Prisoners must not only point out their faults and make self-criticisms, but also "go to the roots", explain "why" they did wrong and "how" they intend to improve their behaviour in future. This process is called "looking at the essence through phenomena". If a prisoner fails to see any misdeeds, the group leader or other inmates may point out faults he or she has overlooked. However, unlike the criticism meetings, organized whenever a prisoner is found to have committed certain misdeeds, the weekly "self-examination" is the occasion for prisoners individually to examine and account for their behaviour. Notes are taken during such meetings and kept on file by the authorities.

In addition, general evaluations of the prisoners' behaviour are made periodically after a more intense process of "mutual and self-examination". The frequency of such evaluations appears to vary from one institution to another. In some places they occur every three months, in others they apparently coincide with the half-yearly or yearly "discipline training" which precedes the formal announcement of rewards and punishments.

These periodical evaluations are the equivalent of mobilization campaigns.[7] They are initiated by the penal institution's director, and all warders and prisoners participate. They may last for several days or weeks and the time for work may be reduced during that period. Generally they include several phases: "self-examination" (*jiantao*), "mutual denunciation" (*jiaodai*), "crime-confession" (*jiao zui*), "admission of guilt" (*renzui*). Prisoners who reveal bad behaviour in the process are subjected to "struggle" sessions.

Former prisoners have reported that, at the end of this process, each prisoner has to write a "self-examination", in a standardized form which must include detailed answers to precise questions on: the acknowledgement of one's crimes, the observance of regulations and discipline, one's attitude at labour and study, reliance upon the Government and one's plans to reform oneself in future.[8] The answers have to be both detailed and factual; for instance, the dates, circumstances and causes of any event reported must be given, as well as the names of people possibly involved. Under the heading "reliance on the Government", prisoners are asked to report the misdeeds committed by others giving, again, names, dates and places. Once completed, these individual evaluations are reviewed in each group; the group's criticisms are incorporated and they are forwarded to the warders. The warders in their turn include their own comments, and the reports are then filed in the prisoners' dossiers.

A prisoner who was held in the *Lianping* camp (Guangdong

province) between 1971 and 1974 told Amnesty International that "denunciation and confession" campaigns took place in the camps whenever a political campaign was launched throughout the country. During such campaigns, "non-reformed" prisoners were singled out and criticized, sometimes severely. According to his account, at such periods, the "middle-brigade" leaders were asked by the camp authorities to look for prisoners in their brigades who "resisted reform" (*kanggai fenzi*). The middle-brigade leaders had first to gather some "materials" (denunciations) about the "resistant" prisoners and to criticize them verbally. These prisoners were taken to "struggle" meetings[9] where an account was given of their "resist-reform" behaviour: this apparently ranged from minor misdemeanours such as refusing to take baths (the camp authorities were apparently keen on hygiene), to acts considered important misdeeds, such as voicing dissatisfaction (*buman yanlun*). Throughout the "one-strike, three-anti" campaign,[10] almost every week some prisoner was subjected to a "struggle" session, during which he was forced to kneel down, humiliated and kicked.

Physical violence towards prisoners during struggle sessions had apparently ended in the *Lianping* camp by 1973-74, and although prisoners were still subjected to criticism for reasons similar to those mentioned above, they were no longer beaten.

The system of mutual reporting helps to create a certain amount of distrust between prisoners and gives the authorities vast powers over them. Prisoners rarely reveal their true thoughts to members of their own group as they can never be sure that the latter will not denounce them in order to achieve "merit" or to mitigate their own punishment if they come under criticism. Equally, if a prisoner is subjected to a "struggle", the whole group has to participate and some prisoners may take advantage of this to give free rein to private resentment.

Relations between prisoners belonging to different groups are equally difficult because their lives are very compartmentalized and regimented. Former prisoners say that free meetings and discussions between inmates are not permitted. If two prisoners are found alone together, talking to one another, they are immediately questioned separately about the conversation. If they cannot justify this, and if their stories are inconsistent, they may be suspected of "counter-revolutionary" activities and severely punished.

Even so, the strict control and the system of mutual surveillance do not prevent friendships between prisoners. The shared hardship of reform through labour and the common knowledge that whatever they do or say will be considered unfavourably by the authorities unless they belittle themselves and state that in all circumstances the "Government is right", create a sense of solidarity between prisoners, despite the impossibility of speaking freely.

Methods of political education and thought-reform are similar in all penal institutions, but vary in emphasis according to the prisoners' category. Non-convicted offenders held in detention centers spend most of their time in study and discussions related to confessions, whereas convicted prisoners who work in labour-reform brigades discuss for the most part problems centering on work. Major convicted offenders in prisons are subjected to a more intense program of political education and ideological reform; much time is spent in reviewing their past life and crimes, writing autobiographies and making repeated confessions.

Releases

Prison and camp administrators often remind prisoners that their sentences are "flexible" and that if they reform themselves quickly they may be granted an early release. On the other hand, bad behaviour—or, in official terms, "resistance to reform despite repeated education"—may be punished by an increased sentence. Acts classified as "resistant" include failure to fulfil production norms for several months in succession, repeated violations of disciplinary rules or "sabotage" (damaging equipment).

According to former prisoners, reduction of sentences is rather rare and is used mainly to create "typical examples" of "good" behaviour. Increases in sentences are apparently slightly more frequent. Generally the severity of the authorities towards "resistant" prisoners appears to exceed their leniency towards those who behave well. Additional sentences for "bad" behaviour include those imposed on prisoners who are retried for committing in detention acts considered criminal: acts of violence, attempts to escape or "spreading counter-revolutionary propaganda or rumours"—which may amount simply to voicing critical remarks about one's treatment or about the Party and the authorities.

The date of release therefore depends on behaviour in detention. The Law on Reform Through Labour specifies that offenders "who should be released" are to be given a certificate of release which includes a general evaluation of their behaviour, and money for travelling home.[11]

However, not all prisoners are allowed to return to their place of origin, or to choose their employment freely after release. When the Law on Reform Through Labour was adopted in 1954, the Government at the same time issued regulations about release, called

"Provisional Measures for Dealing with the Release of Reform Through Labour Criminals at the Expiration of their Term of Imprisonment and for Placing Them and Getting Them Employment".[12] They specified that the reform through labour bodies could "retain", place and find employment for offenders due for release in any one of the following circumstances:

1. when they themselves want to stay in the labour-reform brigade and get employment, and are needed for reform through labour production;
2. if they have no home to return to and no chance of employment;
3. if they are criminals who have undergone reform through labour in sparsely populated districts and, at the end of their term of imprisonment, are needed to join settlers, to found a family, and stay where they are.[13]

A number of ex-convicts do "choose" to remain in the labour-reform institutions after release, but, according to former prisoners, they usually do so for fear of discrimination against them in society, or because they would be an embarrassment to their families, or because the organization for which they worked previously refuses to take them back. Their choice is, in fact, limited by the way society regards ex-convicts and by the fact that they cannot seek employment freely.

The Provisional Measures indicate that only those "whose reform through labour was relatively good, who have production skills and are needed by enterprises and departments for social production" may be encouraged or helped to get jobs.[14]

Other prisoners have no choice: the decision to retain or allocate them is taken by the penal institution administrators and needs only the approval of the Public Security agency in charge of review. According to the Provisional Measures for Release, they may be allocated in two ways: either they are employed in a labour-reform unit, which may be the one where they have served their sentence or, if they are not needed there, in another labour-reform institution; or they are assigned to cultivating land set aside for collective production within or near a labour-reform farm[15] —in which case they may either be organized in teams working apart from prisoners in the farm or live in a "new village" near it. From then on, they earn a salary related to their work and skills and may be permitted to settle with their families or to marry.[16]

Ex-convicts are bound to accept their assignments. Although they have more freedom of movement than prisoners, they are not allowed to leave the penal institution or "new village" without permission, nor to seek employment elsewhere. Moreover, their civil rights are not necessarily restored at the end of their sentences. It is reported that offenders who were originally sentenced as "counter-revolutionary" are particularly likely to be deprived of civil rights for periods usually exceeding their term of imprisonment. Until these rights are restored, they still wear the "cap" of "counter-revolutionary" and are subjected to certain forms of discrimination.

"Retained" ex-prisoners are called by various names: *liuchang renyuan*, "stay longer" or "retained" personnel; *xinsheng renyuan*, "new life" or "reborn" personnel; *nongchang nongong*, "state farm agricultural worker"; *zhigong*, "hired worker". The term "free-workers" has been used frequently outside China for "retained" ex-convicts and, for convenience, is used in this report.

Amnesty International does not know what proportion of prisoners is released (unconditionally) and what proportion is "retained". It seems, however, that the practice of "retaining" ex-convicts is wide-spread and that their assignment is decided on a case by case basis. They are "retained" for both economic and political reasons. "Free-workers" constitute a disciplined labour-force which can more easily be sent to development areas than civilians. In addition, in penal institutions they serve a useful purpose by, to some extent, acting as intermediaries between the prisoners and the administration. They often work in the service departments: kitchen, laundry, transport section, repair shops, etc.

According to former prisoners, the practice of "retaining" ex-convicts is also due to official concern about preventing "adverse effects" on society. It is sometimes assumed that habitual (criminal) offenders may resume their criminal activities if released and that they constitute a "danger to society". The same applies to political offenders who, furthermore, are more likely than criminal offenders to claim after release that they were wrongly sentenced, particularly if, in the meantime, the official political "line" has changed.

Amnesty International has received information about "free-workers" retained in penal institutions against their will. In one such case, a carpenter from Canton named Hu, who became a "free-worker" in 1970, is said to have committed suicide after despairing of ever being allowed to return to normal life. He had served a seven-year sentence in a labour camp in Huaiji county (Guangdong province), having been arrested in Canton in 1963 and accused of being an active "counter-revolutionary". Originally from Taiping county (Guangdong), he had been working since 1949 in one of the corporations, originally private, which survived after Liberation and were gradually transformed or integrated into state-owned enterprises. Hu was the leader of a group of free woodworkers and had apparently achieved some influence through his profession. This is said to have been the main reason for his arrest. In 1963, he was charged with "leading a counter-revolutionary gang", sentenced to 20 years' labour-reform and sent to the Huaiji camp. However, his sentence was later reduced to seven years—apparently a partial acknowledgement that he had been falsely accused, as such a reduction of sentence is very unusual. At the end of his sentence Hu was "retained" in the camp as a "free-worker". He earned about 30 *yuan* a month and worked in the camp kitchen and repair shops. From then on, visits from relatives were authorized frequently and his family could have had permission to settle with him in the camp. However, it appears that Hu hoped to be allowed to return to Canton and discouraged his relatives from joining him. More than a year after becoming a "free-worker", he is reported to have committed suicide, having apparently lost all hope of ever leaving the camp.

Most "free-workers" live in "dormitories" (*sushe*) in prison blocks or farm quarters reserved for them. Their work conditions are similar to those of prisoners, and they have to attend the same sort of study sessions and participate in ideological campaigns. They have certain social benefits (free medical care, free housing, free entertainment), but their wages are lower than those prevailing outside penal institutions.

In the *Baoanzhao* labour-reform farm of Heilongjiang province, the "free-workers' " monthly wages were said to be, in 1972, as follows:

— head of the "free-workers" brigade: 40 *yuan;*
— "free-workers" with civil rights: about 35 *yuan*;
— "free-workers" without civil rights: between 22 and 31 *yuan*, depending on the type of work, output and the worker's political attitude;
— old or weak "free-workers" undertaking light work: between 12 and 18 *yuan*.

The basic food available at the free-workers' collective canteen cost between 12 and 14 *yuan* a month, which was automatically deducted from their pay according to the following system: each person was given ration tickets (*liangpiao*) which they exchanged for food every day. The tickets were counted regularly and the equivalent money deducted from pay. The ration tickets were printed by the free-workers' unit and therefore could not be used anywhere else. The free-workers' farm also had a small store more than two miles away from the barracks. Every fortnight, on their day off, two or three people had to do the shopping for all the free-workers in a "company" (*pai*), and the group leaders kept the accounts for free-workers in their respective groups.

The *Baoanzhao* farm is one of the reclamation farms established in sparsely inhabited areas where free-workers' dependants have been encouraged to settle. The free-workers' families on this farm came mainly from Shandong, Jiangsu, Hunan, Hubei and Zhejiang provinces. It is reported that wives who chose to join their husbands did so because they were in a difficult economic situation and had been politically ostracized in their home provinces. Many prisoners' wives, in fact, divorce their husbands long before the latter are released in order to avoid discrimination and ensure a normal life for their children.

The conditions of the free-workers' families on the *Baoanzhao* farm have been described to Amnesty International as slightly better than those of single "free-workers". Whereas the latter live collectively, free-workers with dependants live in special quarters where individual rooms with kitchen facilities are provided for each family. Wives may work and earn between 10 and 30 *yuan* a month. Food is sold to them by the brigade. Their ration of carbohydrates is fixed at about 30 *catties* per person per month—slightly less for the children.

After the Cultural Revolution, the lives of "free-workers'" families changed: they are said to have been gathered together in a special brigade, away from the rest of the camp, in which husbands and wives worked separately. The "free-workers relatives' group" (*zhigong jiashu xiaozu*) was given land which they cultivated on their own. The organization of their work and the system for evaluating it was different from the free-workers', and this was meant "to draw the class line" between ex-convicts—suspected of exerting a pernicious influence—and their relatives. Children who graduated from junior high school were organized as a "youth team" (*qingnian dui*) which also worked on its own.

It has been reported that some children were gathered together in a special "youth team" living quite apart from their parents, apparently because the authorities considered the latter "stubborn reactionaries". They were educated carefully and told that the Government did not confuse them with their "reactionary" parents. The authorities encouraged them to demonstrate that, politically and at work, they could do better than their parents, warned them "not to mix with the four bad elements" and told them "not to protect" their parents. As a result, some of the children came to despise their parents and denounced them. Several such cases have been reported to Amnesty International.

One case involved a former hospital director from Shanghai who was denounced by his daughter at the end of the Cultural Revolution for listening to "enemy radio broadcasts". He had until then had a privileged position in the camp. Arrested during the Land Reform

(1950-51), he became a "free-worker" in 1957 and was put in charge of a branch-farm hospital ward. His high qualifications were rewarded by unusually high pay: 70 to 80 *yuan* a month. He was never criticized and enjoyed privileges not usually accorded to free-workers, such as eating with the cadres. After his daughter denounced him, he was transferred to the "free-worker" agricultural brigade and his pay was downgraded to about 30 *yuan* a month. As he was not accustomed to manual labour, the quality of his work was below average and his health is said to have been affected.

Free-workers are not allowed to exercise parental authority and they may be punished for simply scolding their children. The family of a teacher from Hunan province, Zhou Paichi, is reported to have been split up after one such incident during the Cultural Revolution. Zhou had become a "free-worker" in 1962 after serving a 10-year sentence, and his wife and son came to join him in 1963. The son, who was in his late teens, never addressed Zhou as "father". He never called him by his name either but used the word "*wei*", which is equivalent to "hey". One day Zhou angrily told his son to call him by his name. The incident was reported and brought about the separation of the family.

Ex-prisoners have reported that the practice of "retaining" offenders at the end of their sentences is widespread and affects equally those sentenced to labour-reform and those "assigned" to labour-rehabilitation. The discipline to which they are subjected and the fact that they are often treated as second-class citizens makes their life very much like that of prisoners.

Amnesties

There has been only one general amnesty in the People's Republic of China since 1949. It was declared by Presidential Order[17] on 17 September 1959 to commemorate the 10th anniversary of the founding of the PRC. The amnesty was to apply to the following categories of prisoners: "war criminals", "counter-revolutionary criminals" and "ordinary" (common-law) criminals. In all cases there was a condition: the prisoners concerned were to be those who had "really reformed from evil to good". The provisions of the Amnesty Order were as follows:

"1. War criminals from the Jiang Jieshi [Chiang Kai-shek] clique [18] and from the puppet Manzhouguo[19] who have already served 10 years in custody and who have really reformed from evil to good shall be released.

2. Counter-revolutionary criminals sentenced to five years or less who have already served half of their sentence and have really

reformed, and those sentenced to more than five years who have already served two-thirds of their sentence and have really reformed from evil to good, shall be released.

3. Ordinary [common-law] criminals sentenced to five years or less who have already served one-third of their sentence and really reformed, and those sentenced to more than five years who have already served half of their sentence and really reformed from evil to good, shall be released.

4. Criminals sentenced to death with suspension of execution for two years who have already served one year of the suspension and really reformed shall have their sentence reduced to a minimum of 15 years or life imprisonment.

5. Criminals sentenced to life imprisonment who have already served seven years and have demonstrated that they have really reformed shall have their sentence reduced to a minimum of 10 years."

It is clear that the provisions of the Amnesty Order were more favourable to "ordinary" (common-law) offenders than to "counter-revolutionaries".

The Order was to be executed by the Supreme People's Court and the High People's Courts. The total number of prisoners who were released or had their sentences reduced under the amnesty is not known, but some figures are available. According to Bao Ruowang, by the end of 1959 a total of 12,082 people had been amnestied, including 2,424 "counter-revolutionaries" and 9,269 ordinary criminals.[20] Jerome Cohen cites a report from the *Henan Daily* of 1 March 1960, according to which 4,263 people were released and 294 had their sentences reduced in Henan province.[21]

When the general amnesty of prisoners was decreed in 1959, steps were taken also to deal with the "rightists". On 16 September 1959, the CCP Central Committee and the State Council jointly adopted a "Decision on the Question of Dealing with Rightists who Really Demonstrate their Reform".[22] The Decision stipulated that all "rightist elements who had already reformed from evil to good and who demonstrated in words and deeds that they had really reformed" should no longer be treated as bourgeois rightists and should have their rightist "caps" removed. The removal of the "cap" did not necessarily mean release from labour-rehabilitation camps. The Decision stated that the "units in which they were located" were to summarize the results of their performance in work and study and announce it to the "masses". It did not say whether they would be allowed to return to their original place of work or residence. Further-more, the removal of the "rightist" label was conditional on good behaviour.

The number of rightists who were actually released as a result of this measure is not known. According to Edgar Snow, in October 1959 the Government announced that the label had been removed from 26,000 rightists. He reports also being told unofficially (in 1960) that this was the "great majority".[23] However, a comparison of this figure with that of 300,000 rightists given in unofficial texts attributed to Mao[24] shows that this was only a small proportion.

As regards "war criminals", according to a Resolution from the State Council,[25] in November 1960 33 war criminals had already been released since the (general) amnesty of September 1959. Special amnesties for war criminals were decreed in 1960, 1961 and 1963 by Presidential Orders and there were reportedly two others up to 1966. According to a former Nationalist official, Duan Kewen, who was imprisoned in Fushun until 1975, between 50 and 60 "war criminals" were released from Fushun under the amnesties declared between 1959 and 1966.[26] More recently, several groups of high-ranking officials from the former Guomindang administration, most of whom were arrested about 1950, were released by special amnesty in 1974 and 1975. These amnesties were publicly announced and are apparently the only ones to have been declared since the Cultural Revolution.

Notes

1 Emphasis added.

2 Act for Reform Through Labour, Article 27.

3 ibid., Article 29; see Chapter III, p.

4 Apart from individual accounts published by former prisoners (some are cited in Chapter III, p. 95), one study based on prisoners' testimonies gives detailed information on the "thought reform" process in the PRC: *Thought Reform and the Psychology of Totalism: A Study of "Brainwashing" in China*, by Robert Jay Lifton, Pelican Books, 1967.

5 See p. 140.

6 About cell leaders, see, for instance, Rickett, op. cit., pp. 158-160.

7 Examples from prisoners' testimonies have been given in Cohen, op. cit., p. 260 and White, op. cit., p. 197. See also Bao Ruowang, op. cit., pp. 150-155 and Duan Kewen, op. cit., 28 and 29 October 1976.

8 See the example of self-evaluation given by Bao Ruowang, ibid., pp. 151-155.

9 See Chapter IV, pp. 128-129, about "struggle" meetings.

10 See Chapter I, p.12, and Chapter II, p. 45, for details on this campaign.

11 Act for Reform Through Labour, Article 61.

12 Adopted 26 August 1954, promulgated 7 September 1954. The Provisional Measures have been published in *Zhongyang Renmin Zhengfu Faling Huipian* (1954), Peking, 1955, pp. 44-45; translation in Cohen, op. cit., pp. 634-635.

13 Provisional Measures for Release, Article 2.

14 ibid., Article 5, paragraph 1.

15 ibid., Article 5, paragraphs 2 and 3, and Article 8.

16 ibid., Article 5, paragraph 2, and Article 7.

17 Amnesty Order of the President of the PRC, declared 17 September 1959, in *Zhonghua Renmin Gongheguo Fagui Huipian* (July-December 1959), Vol, 10, pp. 58-59. The Order was issued after the NPC Standing Committee approved the amnesty on the recommendation of the CCP Central Committee.

18 This refers to members of the former Nationalist (Guomindang) Government, army and administration.

19 The Manzhouguo (state of Manchuria) was created in 1932 as a Japanese protectorate after Japan invaded the north of China. In 1934 it became an Empire when the Japanese placed at its head Pu Yi, the former Manchu Emperor. Pu Yi and other Manchu officials were imprisoned after 1949 in the Fushun War Criminal Center.

20 Bao Ruowang, op. cit., p. 162.

21 Cohen, op. cit., p. 631.

22 In *Zhonghua Renmin Gongheguo Fagui Huipian,* Vol. 10, pp. 61-62.

23 Snow, op cit., p. 389.

24 See Chapter I, pp. 28-29.

25 Resolution From The State Council Regarding the Amnesty of War Criminals Who Have Already Really Reformed, 17 November 1960, in *Zhonghua Renmin Gongheguo Fagui Huipian*, Vol. 12 pp. 67-68.

26 See Duan Kewen, op. cit., 23 December 1976.

Lin Xiling

In 1957, the year of her arrest, Lin Xiling was a fourth-year law student at China People's University in Peking and a Party member.

Lin Xiling came from a poor family and had received only an elementary education before she entered university. When she was 15, she joined a People's Liberation Army art group, leaving it in 1953 with the qualification of "cultural teacher". She was then allowed to enter university on the recommendation of the Party and was admitted to China People's University in 1953.

In 1955, literary circles in China were divided on the question of Hu Feng, a prominent Chinese writer who had come under attack for criticizing the literary standards set up by the Chinese Communist Party. A press campaign to criticize Hu Feng (who was subsequently arrested) was launched in the spring of 1955 and followed by a new campaign against "counter-revolutionaries". These two campaigns alienated many members of the intelligentsia and, two years later, the CCP decided to allow them to voice their complaints by launching a campaign to "rectify the Party's style of work". This campaign is better known as the "Hundred Flowers" movement.[1] The rectification campaign was officially launched on 30 April 1957 and in May open debates on the "style of work" of the Party began among students, intellectuals, journalists, etc., many of whom soon voiced strong criticisms of the CCP.

At Peking University, students participated in the same way in the movement and Lin Xiling was one of the most outspoken critics. In her speeches, she defended Hu Feng, questioning the credibility of the charge that he was a "counter-revolutionary". She observed that the liberal policy towards writers that Hu Feng had advocated, and for which he was criticized and arrested in 1955, was now being implemented by the CCP itself. She also criticized more generally the policy of "suppression of counter-revolutionaries" as well as the system of privileges based on political alignment and the lack of democracy in Chinese society.[2]

As such fundamental criticisms were being expressed, the "Hundred Flowers" movement was abruptly stopped in early June 1957. On 8 June, the official press started counter-attacking the critics and stigmatized them as "rightists". An "anti-rightist" campaign was subsequently launched throughout the country and the more outspoken critics of the CCP were arrested, while others—who repudiated their views—were simply criticized publicly.

Lin Xiling was among those arrested. Her name was mentioned on several occasions in the official press during the "anti-rightist" campaign. On 28 June 1957, for instance, the New China News Agency reported that, during a meeting of the Communist Youth League in Peking, "Hung Yu-chung, a student of China People's University, was a little abashed at first when she made her speech, for, deceived by Lin Hsi-ling [Lin Xiling], a rightist in the University, she had once lost her way and waved a banner and raised war-cries in union with the rightists. But since the exposure of Lin's rumours and false accusations, Hung has come back to herself."[3]

No official information was ever disclosed about the fate of Lin Xiling, but her case was mentioned officially as being one of "contradiction between the people and the enemy", which indicates that she was tried and sentenced. The daily newspaper Guangming Ribao of 3 September 1961 quoted Foreign Minister Chen Yi as saying: "As for the rightists Lin Xiling and Tan Tianrong,[4] they are a different kind of people. The contradiction between them and us is one between ourselves and the enemy."[5]

Lin Xiling is reported to have first been detained in Peking Prison No. 1 and later sent to a labour camp. The location of the camp is not known. According to a Chinese student who was in Peking in 1966, she had been sentenced to 20 years' imprisonment with deprivation of civil rights for life and was still detained at the time of the Cultural Revolution. Other sources have also reported that she was still imprisoned in the mid 1970s. Her present fate is unknown.

Notes

1 See Chapter I, pp. 17-18.

2 Two speeches made by Lin Xiling at that time are published in Dennis J. Doolin's book, *Communist China, the Politics of Student Opposition*, Stanford University, 1964.

3 "Members of Chinese Young Communist League of Higher Institutions in the Capital Resolve to Struggle to the Last against Rightists", New China News Agency, Peking, 28 June 1957 (in *Survey of China, Mainland Press*, No. 1595, pp. 32-33).

4 Tan Tianrong was a student at Peking University who also took an active part in the "Hundred Flowers" movement.

5 Quoted in Doolin, op. cit., pp. 14-15.

APPENDIX II

Wang Mingdao

Wang Mingdao, a Chinese Protestant pastor, imprisoned continuously since 1957 because of his religious beliefs, will now, if still alive, be 78 years old.[1]

Wang Mingdao was born in 1900 in Peking, where he received primary and high school education until the age of 18. He was baptized while at school and became increasingly interested in religion and theology, deciding at one point to become a preacher. In October 1924 he started holding Bible classes in his home in Peking and he travelled all over China in the years that followed, expressing his religious views to foreign missions and to various Chinese church groups. He married in 1928 and had a son two years later. During this period he wrote several booklets and contributed to a periodical launched in 1927, entitled *Spiritual Food Quarterly*. Finally he decided to open a permanent place of worship in Peking and in 1936 a church was built, which he called "The Christian Tabernacle". In the following years, he continued preaching in Peking and travelled occasionally to the provinces, attracting more followers to his independent church.

Soon after the establishment of the People's Republic of China in 1949, the new authorities invited Chinese church leaders to a conference in Peking, asking them to purge their churches of foreign "imperialist influences" and to cooperate with the new Government. In July 1951 the "Three Self-Reform Movement" of Peking churches was founded at the inspiration of the Government, with, as its main objectives:

1. opposition to imperialism and severance of relations between Chinese churches and churches abroad
2. support of the Three Self-Reform Movement initiated in Shanghai
3. propagation of patriotic education.

This was at the time of the Korean war and the whole population was mobilized under the slogan "Resist America and Aid Korea".

These requirements were an important step towards limiting the independence of the churches and freedom of worship. Some Chinese Christian leaders consequently refused to join the Three Self-Reform Movement, maintaining that their churches had been organized by Chinese Christians and had always been independent of foreign missions. Wang Mingdao was among those who refused to join for several years.

Wang Mingdao's uncompromising stand on the independence of the Church led to his first arrest in 1955. Before this, a campaign to criticize him was launched and "accusation meetings" were held against him in various cities. When he was arrested in August 1955, three charges were brought against him:

– opposing the government by injuring the Three Self-Reform Movement
– preaching anti-government statements which hindered the Land Reform and the "Resist America, Aid Korea" movements
– collaborating with American imperialists.

This third accusation appears, in fact, to have been based merely on his relationship with American friends before 1949.

During detention, Wang finally, under pressure, signed a confession and, together with his wife who had also been arrested, was released a few months later. Afterwards he showed signs of severe strain for a while, being totally demoralized by his recantation. However, later he is reported to have informed the authorities that his confession had been made under duress and did not represent his true opinions.

Probably because of this, he was re-arrested in 1957 during the nationwide campaign against "rightists". His case was mentioned on 2 August 1957 by the New China News Agency, the official press agency of the PRC. The NCNA reported a statement made by patriotic Christians, according to which attempts had been made by certain Christians to reopen the case of Wang Mingdao, who was described as a "counter-revolutionary who had donned the cloak of religion".[2] He has been in prison ever since. It is reported that he was first sentenced to 15 years' imprisonment, but retried in 1963, when his original sentence was increased to life imprisonment. No official information was ever given about his trial. He was reported to be still imprisoned in Peking in 1966 and to have been transferred to a labour camp in Dadong (northern Shānxi province) in 1970. According to one source, he was still alive and in detention in 1974. His present fate and whereabouts are unknown.

Notes

1 Published information about Wang Mingdao is available in Leslie Lyall's *Three of China's Mighty Men*, London, 1973, and in *China Notes*, Vol. I, No 1, September 1962 (a journal sponsored by the China Committee of the National Council of Churches in the USA).

2 NCNA, 2 August 1957, in SWB, No. 692, 22 August 1957, p. 23.

APPENDIX III

Chamba Lobsang

The information below was given to Amnesty International by a Tibetan exile who claimed to have been a direct witness of the events reported. Although not in a position to verify the accuracy of the report, Amnesty International is concerned about the allegations made in it regarding the circumstances in which a group of Tibetans were detained in 1959 and sentenced to life imprisonment in 1960 in Shekar district (Autonomous Region of Tibet). The following is a summary of the report.

In 1959, Chamba Lobsang, aged about 26, was a monk in the Shekar Chode Monastery in Shekar district, south-west of Lhasa (the capital of the Autonomous Region of Tibet). Chamba Lobsang was a *Linka Tulku*, living in a small "retreat" (*Linka*) near the monastery. In Tibetan Buddhism, a *Tulku* is a religious figure, believed to be re-incarnated in "saints" and ascetics.

According to Tibetan administrative custom, Shekar district was then administered by two District Commissioners, one lay and one representing the religious authority.

In March 1959, a rebellion against the Chinese authorities broke out in Lhasa. About two months later, in May or June 1959, the area surrounding the Shekar Chode Monastery was encircled by troops of the Chinese People's Liberation Army (PLA). The area included the main monastery, the *Linka* retreat, a village of some 400 families and a supply depot of the "old" Tibetan Army's Dingri Division (which housed a garrison of 100 Tibetan soldiers).[The refugee who reported this case to Amnesty International did not indicate whether the Dingri Division had been engaged in fighting against the Chinese troops.]

After surrounding the area, the Chinese commander called for six people to surrender themselves at the headquarters of the Chinese camp: three officials of the Shekar Chode Monastery (including the Abbot), the two District Commissioners and the commanding officer of the Dingri Division supply depot. The Dingri Division was asked to surrender its arms and offer no resistance. This was done and all munitions were handed over to the Chinese forces. The Chinese forces then withdrew, but took with them the Tibetan commanding officer, the 100 men of the Dingri Division and the District Commissioner who represented the religious authority. Before leaving the area, they released the four other detainees (the three monastery officials and the lay District Commissioner) and told them that all aspects of the traditional administration could continue in the normal way (including the traditional system of justice) and that there would be no reforms in the district for the next three years. After they left, no Chinese were seen in the area for the next three months.

About October 1959, however, a PLA unit of 200 men, accompanied by members of the Public Security Department of the Autonomous Region of Tibet, arrived at the Monastery. They arrested the three monastery officials and the lay District Commissioner, who were questioned for 11 days in the vacant residence of the "religious" District Commissioner (who had been taken away previously).

At the end of the 11 days, the Chinese Command called a meeting of all the monks in the monastery and announced that the four detainees had signed statements of self-criticism and that the entire area had been declared "reactionary". All monastery and locally-owned properties were to be confiscated, the monastery was to be closed and the traditional administrative system was to cease functioning.

During the meeting, a list of 37 names was read out. It included several monastery officials, monks and two lay district officials who were present at the meeting. They were told that they were scheduled for a "re-education" program lasting seven to 15 days. After they had gathered some clothing and bedding, the 37 people were taken to the former office of the District Commissioners.

They were held in this improvised place of detention for the next six months. During this time, they were joined by others, mostly ordinary people, until they were 69 in number. They were questioned about their past and asked to write self-criticisms, starting with a review of their lives from the age of eight until the time the PLA arrived in their district. They were kept in the main hall of the building, but individual questioning took place in the surrounding small rooms.

Various means were used to extract confessions from those who refused to cooperate with their interrogators, including, it is alleged, the use of handcuffs (which could tighten with movements of the wrists); confinement in tiny cells (not wide enough to sit or sleep in easily and not high enough to stand upright in); and, in some cases, "struggle" sessions, at which villagers from other areas were assembled for the occasion and encouraged to beat the detainees who were the object of the "struggle".

By April 1960, all those detained in the Shekar District Commissioners' Office had "confessed" under pressure. A public meeting was then organized, presided over by the Chinese commander. Each detainee was called up on to a platform, and stood there while the confession was read out; then the accusations and sentence were announced. The *Linka Tulku*, Chamba Lobsang, was reported to have been accused of exploiting the masses in the name of religion and was sentenced to life imprisonment. Six other people are reported to have been sentenced to life imprisonment during this meeting: Lobsang Choempel (Steward of Estate), Chanchub Tsultim (monk), Lungtok Choempel (monk), Menri Dogyal (lay District Commissioner), Thundup Chokpa (farmer) and Tenzim (secretary).

On the same day, the 69 condemned men were taken to Shigatse (west of Lhasa) in a convoy of four trucks and put in Karkang prison, previously a large grain storage warehouse. After five months there, they were moved to Ngari prison, about three miles away but within the administrative jurisdiction of Karkang.

Ngari prison was near an agricultural project where the prisoners, split up into small groups, carried out compulsory labour. The seven prisoners serving life imprisonment were still in Ngari prison in 1964, as well as others from Shekar district who got shorter sentences and should by now be released. Their present fate is unknown.

APPENDIX IV

Deng Qingshan

Deng Qingshan's background and the circumstances which led to his arrest during the 1970 "one-strike, three-anti" campaign were described earlier.[1] Information about his case was published in 1976 in *Huang He*, a Chinese-language review published in Hong Kong.[2] The account below is based on this report and on additional information given by direct witnesses of the affair. Although Amnesty International is not in a position to check the specific details of this account, similar cases of arbitrary arrest at that period have been reported and some accounts of the "one-strike, three-anti" campaign elsewhere are like this one.

In 1970, shortly after the "one-strike, three-anti" campaign began in his production brigade, Deng Qingshan was made the "target" of the campaign because of his "bad" background. This decision was taken by the brigade's cadres and was not made public. It was the outcome of three days of meetings between the following people:

the brigade's Party members

members of the "Security Protection Committee"

the production teams' leaders (rural brigades are subdivided into production teams)

members of the Youth League (the youth organization of the Communist Party)

the brigade's political propagandist (*Maozidong fudaoyuan*).

After these meetings, an investigation team was formed in the brigade, comprising the Party Secretary, the head of the Security Protection Committee, the head of the militia, some members of the "team in charge of carrying out the class struggle" (*douchadui*) and some people responsible for taking notes.

They all settled in Deng's production team for a few days. Members of the team first talked to individual "poor peasants" and "activists" about the class struggle and the need to find class enemies. Soon their actions and speeches created a tense atmosphere in the production team. People did not know exactly who was going to be the "victim" but understood clearly that it was a serious affair. The team then displayed several slogans: "We should drag out the class enemies" . . . "You had better confess now" . . . "Confession deserves clemency, resistance deserves severity" . . . and "mobilization" continued in various ways. Two or three days later, a big meeting was organized for all members of the production team. They were told that there was a "counter-revolutionary" among them whom everyone should denounce, but the name of the counter-revolutionary was not disclosed. People were frightened and started thinking of what they could report about others. They were asked to write down whatever they knew which seemed wrong to them. Those who could not write well were given help. The meeting lasted a long time because many people who presented their papers to the Party Secretary were told that they were not "good enough" and had to be rewritten.

Finally, 81 denunciation papers were collected; most of them unimportant. However, some of them concerned several young people in the village who, in one of the papers, were accused of having once stolen a fish and were said to be often in Deng's company.

These young men were taken to the brigade's headquarters by the investigation team and a "study class"[3] was organized for them. They were urged to confess their "illicit relationship" with a "counter-revolutionary". As they were unable to say anything, Deng's name was then mentioned and they were asked to say what they knew of him.

Meanwhile, some members of the investigation team went back to the production team to ask the peasants to denounce these young men. The previous process was repeated and in the new denunciations the investigators found accusations against two of the young men. One was denounced for having had an "illicit sexual relationship" with a woman and the other for telling a story to some peasants about the Emperor of the Zhou dynasty and his concubine, from which it was deduced that he compared Mao Tsetung with the tyrannical Emperor and Mao's wife with the cruel concubine.

Once this information was brought back to the brigade, these two young men were taken aside by the investigators. The first was threatened with being labelled a "bad element" unless he made up for his crime by "exposing" Deng. Frightened, he testified that Deng had once told him that Mao had been transformed from a snake into a man, and, every year, had to go swimming at the time when the skin changed. To a Chinese mind, this would sound more like a peasant's story than one told by an educated youth and it seems unlikely that Deng was its author. Nevertheless the statement was written down, signed and finger-printed by the young man. The other young man was in his turn threatened with being branded a "counter-revolutionary" for slandering Chairman Mao with the story of the Zhou Emperor. He then accused Deng of having told the story and he, too, signed and finger-printed a statement. The two of them were then allowed to go home. The other young men who had been taken with them to the brigade were then asked to confirm the charges, which they did, for fear of being kept longer in the "study class". Their testimony was also written down and their finger-prints taken

This completed the first part of the preliminary investigation; the evidence of two "crimes" committed by Deng plus witnesses had been found. The second part began with the return of the investigation team to Deng's production team, where the "masses" were again mobilized. Twelve "poor peasants" were found to confirm the charges against Deng and to give additional details. They also made statements which they signed and finger-printed and a first dossier (*shumian zuixing cailiao*) was written, including the following information:

1. Deng's background and class origin
2. his two "crimes"
3. the places and times at which the "crimes" were committed
4. the witnesses to each of the "crimes"
5. Deng's acceptance or rejection of the above facts.

Deng was then arrested by the militia, taken to the brigade for interrogation and told to confess. He did not yet know precisely what he was accused of. The cadres gave him the dossier to read. Under point 5, he could write either "conforms with the facts" (*shushi*) and "I admit my crimes" (*renzui*) or "does not conform with the facts" (*bu shushi*). Deng was urged to write something. He had, in fact, little choice, because refuting evidence given by 12 "poor peasants" was an impossible challenge and the only other alternative—admitting the crimes— would make him a "counter-revolutionary". At first, therefore, he refused to say or write anything.

A "struggle meeting" was then called—the whole brigade stopped working for an entire day to attend it. Deng was confronted with the young men and the 12 "poor peasants" who had denounced him and who, more than anybody else, were adamant that he should admit the crimes. In this situation nobody would dare to speak in his defence. Deng was pushed, insulted, even beaten and yet did not confess. Finally, the brigade's Party Secretary threatened to write on the dossier that Deng had "resisted to the very end"—a powerful threat in China as the official policy of "leniency to those who confess, severity to those who resist" is well known to everyone. At that point, Deng had no choice but to sign the statement and he wrote "*renzui*" ("I admit my crimes").

A "recommendation for arrest" was then written by the brigade cadres and sent with the dossier to the commune's "Security Defence Group". At the same time Deng was sent to the commune and his case was no longer the responsibility of the brigade cadres.

This was the starting-point of a process of reinvestigation which was carried out in three stages. Investigators from the commune were sent to Deng's production team to interrogate the witnesses, especially about factual inconsistencies in the dossier. The commune's investigators, however, began their investigation by assuring the peasants repeatedly that they were "confident in the masses and in the Party's grass-roots"—a guarantee of protection for the witnesses who confirmed their statements. The dossier on Deng which was finally compiled by the commune contained fewer inconsistencies than the brigade's dossier.

The commune in turn sent its own dossier of recommendations to the county Public Security authorities who, after again investigating the case along the same lines, issued an "arrest warrant". Deng meanwhile had been transferred to the county's detention center and was now formally "arrested". As the case was considered important, the county authorities handed the dossier to the higher authorities in the district (*zhuanqu*).

The third reinvestigation was therefore made by officials from the district Public Security Bureau. This time a more detailed investigation was made. However, in order not to intimidate the witnesses, the district investigators explained again to the peasants that "they were confident in the masses, in the Party's grass-roots and were standing at their side". New details about the crimes were therefore discovered which made the final dossier better and fuller. It was sent by the district to Deng's production brigade for approval. The brigade's Party Secretary and the member responsible for Public Security signed it. The district's dossier did not include the original dossiers prepared by the brigade, commune and county, which were never seen again.

Several months later, preparations were made for passing judgment on Deng. Some officials from the district came to the production brigade for "consultations with the masses", and copies of Deng's dossier were distributed to the production teams. In addition to information about the case, some space was reserved in the dossier for the "opinions of the masses" and for the "opinion of the Party's grass-roots". A meeting was organized for this purpose, but people did not quite know what to say and proposed all sorts of things; some shouted "execution". The brigade's Party Secretary, on the other hand, seemed to feel some remorse and wrote on the dossier: "[Deng] admitted his crimes, cooperative attitude, [he] deserves clemency".

The district officials left the brigade after having collected the "opinions of the masses" and judgment was decided upon outside the brigade. In November 1970, a district Public Security Bureau public notice announced sentences passed on a number of offenders. Deng was on the list. He had been sentenced to 15 years' imprisonment with three years' deprivation of civil rights after release, for slandering Chairman Mao on several occasions between 1967 and 1969. He is reported to have been sent to a labour camp. His present fate is unknown.

Notes

1 See Chapter I, pp. 12-13, for more details on Deng's background and on the "one-strike, three-anti" campaign.

2 "The case of one counter-revolutionary", *Huang He*, No. 1, 1976. Translated in English in the Review *Minus 8*, July-August 1976, and in French in *Esprit*, July-August 1977.

3 See Chapter II, p. 70, note 15, about these "study classes".

Li Zhengtian

In November 1974 a big-character poster was displayed on the walls of Peking Road in Canton (Guangzhou). The poster was unusual on account of its contents and length—it covered about a hundred yards of wall. It was entitled "Concerning Socialist Democracy and Legal System—dedicated to Chairman Mao and the Fourth National People's Congress" and was signed "Li Yizhe".[1]

Li Yizhe is a portmanteau pseudonym made up of parts of the names of the three young men who wrote the poster: *Li* Zhengtian, Chen *Yiy*ang and Wang Xi*zhe*. Li Zhengtian is said to have been the main author.

The first draft of this poster was written in 1973, but Li Zhengtian, together with his friends, later made important changes to the first draft, and the final version, which was displayed publicly in November 1974, included a preface which was longer than the main text of the original article. The poster was photographed by travellers and later translated abroad.

The poster presented a criticism of the "Lin Biao system". Marshal Lin Biao, the former Vice-Chairman of the Party, was reported to have disappeared in September 1971 after an attempted *coup*, and several political campaigns were launched to criticize him between 1972 and 1974.

The authors of the "Li Yizhe" poster stated: "Lin Biao's collapse does not mean an end of his system." They argued that the main task was still to criticize Lin Biao and to repair the injustice done while he was in power:

> "In the summer of 1968, the socialist legal system 'suddenly became inoperative', while, on the other hand, 'the state power is the power to suppress' became operative. All across the land, there were arrests everywhere, suppression everywhere, miscarriages of justice everywhere ...
>
> ". . . among the revolutionaries who put up real fights to oppose the Lin Biao system, not a few had their heads chopped off; and so they are headless; those who were imprisoned are still in prison; and those who were dismissed from office are still suspended."

The poster also listed as follows the demands of the "masses of the people":

> "They demand democracy; they demand a socialist legal system; and they demand the revolutionary rights and the human rights which protect the masses of people."

As can be seen from these extracts, the poster was unusually out-spoken on the subject of the "rights of the people".

After the poster was displayed in the streets of Canton, it was officially criticized in an article collectively written by people in the provincial Propaganda Department. This, too, was displayed and cir-culated in Canton. It was signed *Xuan ji wen* (which literally means "propaganda", "collective", "essay") and attacked the "Li Yizhe" poster on several points.

It is reported that the poster was read also by senior Party leaders in Peking who criticized it as "reactionary and vicious" and represent-ing "bourgeois thought".

Li Zhengtian is said to have been the leader and theoretician of the "Li Yizhe" group and more is known about him than about his two friends. According to various reports, he was born in 1942 in Wuhan, Hubei province (central-east China), and had a "good" family back-ground: several of his relatives were Party members. As a child, Li was sent to study at a famous primary school attached to the Canton Fine Arts College. He graduated from the College and was in his twenties when the Cultural Revolution began (1966).

Like many other young students, he participated actively in the Cultural Revolution in Canton, and was arrested in August 1968 during the waves of arrests which marked the end of it. After being detained for three years in Canton, Li was, according to report, allowed to work in his college library, and continued writing essays and articles on political matters.

The first draft of his essay on "Socialist Democracy and Legal System" was completed by 1973. In the course of the year, Li is reported to have found a room in a house, where he held a few meetings to present his essay. In this way, he gained a certain amount of support. He is also reported to have written many other articles during that period, some of which were reproduced by other people and displayed on lamp-posts in Canton.

In April 1974, an article entitled "Where is Guangdong going?", signed for the first time "Li Yizhe", appeared in the streets of Canton. In the meantime, Li and his two friends had modified the essay on "Socialist Democracy and Legal System" and included in it a strongly-worded preface which was longer than the original text. This final version was posted up in Canton in November 1974, as previously stated, and a criticism of it appeared in the city in early December—the "collective essay" from the province's Propaganda Department. Li replied to the criticism with another article entitled "Please enter the vessel". (This is an approx-imate translation of a Chinese expression referring to a famous

Empress who used to get rid of opponents by having them burnt alive in a large vessel.) The last article he is said to have written was entitled "Farewell to the people of Guangzhou [Canton]."

In December 1974, Li Zhengtian, Chen Yiyang and Wang Xizhe were brought to various institutions in Canton where meetings were organized to criticize them. Such meetings are common in China and vary in importance depending on the case involved. They can be private or public "criticism meetings" and can last for hours, or be repeated for days or weeks if the person concerned does not concede to the criticism. In the case of Li Zhengtian, it is reported that he was allowed to defend his ideas freely and discuss them with his critics.

Wang Xizhe and Chen Yiyang, under pressure during the meetings and perhaps less confident than Li Zhengtian, are reported to have finally given in to the criticism and admitted their "guilt". They were consequently sent to work under surveillance in the countryside in Guangdong province.

Li, it appears, defended his arguments successfully. He is said to have been taken to meetings at the Guangdong province Party school and the Politics Department of Zhongshan (Sun Yat-sen) University in Canton, but was apparently not defeated in argument. "Criticism meetings" were then reportedly held in his absence for a while.

After the Fourth National People's Congress met in Peking in January 1975, the "criticism meetings" against Li stopped in Canton. Sometime in the spring of 1975 Li was sent to work "under the supervision of the masses" in a mine north of Guangdong province. The mine is reported to be in Shaoguan district and to include a mixed labour force of people "under supervision", ordinary workers and prisoners. Li, it was reported, was still working in the mine in 1976.

In early 1977, Li Zhengtian, Chen Yiyang and Wang Xizhe were, according to report, labelled "counter-revolutionary". In June, a traveller to Canton claimed to have seen a notice from Guangdong province High People's Court, announcing that Li Zhengtian had been sentenced to life imprisonment.[2] This report, however, has not been confirmed. It has also been alleged that 10 or 11 people altogether were sentenced in connection with the "Li Yizhe" case with the approval of the central authorities in Peking. Since 1977, the whereabouts of Li, Chen and Wang have not been known, but according to unconfirmed reports, one of them was sent to a labour camp in Yunnan province and the other two to camps in Guangdong province.

Unconfirmed reports in March 1978 said that "Li Yizhe" had been freed; however, by May 1978 Amnesty International had not received confirmation of this release nor any indication that either Li Zhengtian or Chen Yiyang and Wang Xizhe had returned to Canton. According to *Newsweek* of 8 May 1978, the March report about this release had later been disproved.

Notes

1 Li Yizhe, *Guanyu shehuizhuyi de minzhu yu fazhi*, Hong Kong, 1976. Various translations of the poster exist, in particular in *Issues and Studies*, Vol. XII, No. 1, January 1976; *Chinois, si vous saviez . . .*, Paris, 1976; *The Revolution is Dead Long Live the Revolution*, Hong Kong 1976; *China: wer gegen wen?*, Berlin, 1977.

2 See *Far Eastern Economic Review* of 15 July 1977.

INDEX

The letter "n" followed by a number—e.g.: n.16—refers to a note at the end of a chapter and the number immediately preceding the "n" refers to the page on which the note appears (e.g.: 73 n.16).

The number(s) in italics which immediately follow an article or articles of laws refer to the page(s) where the article(s) are mentioned.

A number in brackets after a note—e.g.: n.16 (34)—is the number of the page to which the note refers.

AMNESTY INTERNATIONAL PUBLICATIONS

Report on Allegations of Torture in Brazil, A5, 108 pages, first edition September 1972, re-set with updated preface March 1976: £1.20 (US $3.00).

Report on an Amnesty International Mission to Spain, A5, 24 pages in English, 28 pages Spanish, September 1975: 35 pence (US $0.90).

Prisoners of Conscience in the USSR: Their Treatment and Conditions, A5, 154 pages, November 1975: £1.00 (US $2.50).

AI in Quotes, A5, 24 pages, May 1976, 25 pence (US $0.50).

Amnesty International 1961–1976: A chronology, May 1976: 20 pence (US $0.40).

Professional Codes of Ethics, A5, 32 pages, October 1976: 40 pence (US$1.00).

Report of an Amnesty International Mission to Sri Lanka, A4, 52 pages, second edition December 1976: 75 pence (US $1.25).

Los Abogados Contra La Tortura, A4, 31 pages, first published in Spanish, January 1977: 60 pesetas, 50 pence (US $1.00).

Report on an Amnesty International Mission to the Republic of the Philippines, A5, 60 pages, first published September 1976, second (updated) edition March 1977: £1.00.

Dossier on Political Prisoners Held in Secret Detention Camps in Chile, A4, March 1977: £1,45.

Report of an Amnesty International Mission to Argentina, A4, 92 pages, March 1977: £1.00.

Torture in Greece: The First Torturers' Trial 1975, A5, 98 pages, April 1977: 85 pence.

Islamic Republic of Pakistan. An Amnesty International Report including the findings of a Mission, A4, 96 pages, May 1977: 75 pence.

Evidence of Torture: Studies by the Amnesty International Danish Medical Group, A5, 40 pages, June 1977: 50 pence.

Report of an Amnesty International Mission to The Republic of Korea, A4, 46 pages, first published April 1976, second edition June 1977: 75 pence.

The Republic of Nicaragua. An Amnesty International Report including the findings of a Mission to Nicaragua 10–15 May 1976, A4, 75 pages, July 1977: 75 pence.

Indonesia. An Amnesty International Report, A5, 148 pages, October 1977: £2.00.

Amnesty International Report 1977, A5, 352 pages, December 1977: £2.00.

174

Political Imprisonment in South Africa, A5, 105 pages, January 1978: £1.00.

In addition to these major reports, Amnesty International also publishes a monthly **Newsletter**, an annual **Report** and a series of **Amnesty International Briefing Papers**:

Amnesty International Briefing Papers: a series of human rights reference booklets on individual countries, averaging between 12 and 16 papers in A5 format. Briefing Papers Number 1-14:

Singapore	Malawi	Taiwan (Republic of China)
Paraguay*	Guatemala*	Czechoslovakia*
Iran	Turkey	German Democratic
Namibia	People's Democratic	Republic* (GDR)
Rhodesia/	Republic of Yemen	Morocco
Zimbabwe	*also available in Spanish	

Subscription price for series of 10 Briefing Papers: £6.00 (US $15). Price includes postage and packing. Single copies 40 pence (US $1.00), plus 20 pence (50 cents) for postage and handling.

Amnesty International Newsletter and annual Report: The **Newsletter** is a six-page monthly account of Amnesty International's work for human rights in countries throughout the world and includes a two-page bulletin on the work of the Campaign for the Abolition of Torture. The annual **Report** gives a country-by-country survey of human rights violations which have come to the attention of Amnesty International. Yearly subscription £6.00 (US $15.00) inclusive.

FRENCH and ENGLISH:

Belgium: Amnesty International Belgique, rue Royale 185, 1030 Bruxelles
Canada: Amnistie Internationale, François Martin, 3836 St Hubert Street, Montreal, Quebec H2L 4A5
France: Amnesty International, Section française, 18 rue de Varenne, 75007 Paris
Luxembourg: Amnesty International Luxembourg, Boîte Postale 1914, Luxembourg-Gare
Switzerland: Amnesty International, Suisse Romande, Boîte Postale 1051, CH-3001 Bern

GERMAN and ENGLISH:

Germany, Federal Republic: Amnesty International Sektion der Bundesrepublik, Deutschland e.V., Venusbergweg 48, 5300 Bonn
Austria: Amnesty International, Osterreichische Sektion, Franz Hochedlingergasse 6/22, A-1020 Wien
Switzerland: Amnesty International, Sektion der Schweiz, Postfach 1051, CH-3001 Bern

GREEK and ENGLISH:

Greece: Amnesty International, Greek Section, 22 Kleitomachou Street, Athens 501

ITALIAN and ENGLISH:

Italy: Amnesty International, Italian Section, Via della Penna 51, Rome

JAPANESE and ENGLISH:

Japan: Amnesty International, Japanese Section, Room 74, 3-18 Nishi-Waseda 2-chome, Shinjuku-ku, Tokyo 160

NORWEGIAN and ENGLISH:

Norway: Amnesty International, Norwegian Section, Akersgaten 39 II, Oslo 1

SPANISH and ENGLISH:

Costa Rica: Publicaciones Amnistía Internacional (PAI), Apartado 6306, San José
Spain: Secretariado de la Sección de España, Rambla del Prat 21, Barcelona 12
(Madrid): Columela 2, 1º-der, Madrid 1
(San Sebastián): Apartado 1109, San Sebastián
Venezuela: Amnesty International, Venezuelan Section, Apartado 51184, Caracas 105

SWEDISH and ENGLISH:

Sweden: Amnesty International, Smålandsgatan 2, 114 34 Stockholm